APPEASEMENT

A Study in Political Decline
1933—1939

by

A. L. ROWSE

'Do you not know, my son, with how little
wisdom the world is governed ?'

OXENSTIERNA

The Norton Library

W · W · NORTON & COMPANY · INC ·

NEW YORK

First published in the Norton Library 1963

IN MEMORY

OF

SIR LEWIS NAMIER

COMPANION IN THOSE CAMPAIGNS

Books That Live

The Norton imprint on a book means that in the publisher's
estimation it is a book not for a single season but for the years.
W. W. Norton & Company, Inc.

SBN 393-00139-3

PRINTED IN THE UNITED STATES OF AMERICA

6 7 8 9 0

PREFACE

I HAVE had some difficulty in persuading myself to publish this little book, though I have long intended to write
it. Some indication of this is that two years have passed
since I wrote it. Meanwhile, there is the advantage that
the chief characters have now passed from my small stage.
In their day, however, they took a leading part upon a
much bigger one.

Oxford, it seems, is always news. And the very success-
ful propagators of the idea of the Establishment — a
concept which has now spread round the world — have
assiduously drawn attention to the peculiar position they
consider All Souls College to occupy in it. As usual in
such matters, the public is twenty and thirty years behind
the times.

In the dreadful decade that led 'with the certainty of a
somnambulist' — survivors will recognise the phrase from
its presiding genius — in the decade that led straight to the
war, it is true that a number of Fellows of All Souls were
very prominent and powerful in the nation's affairs. But
it is equally true that a majority of the Fellows, particularly of the younger generation, as we were then, were
strongly opposed to the whole policy and course of

conduct with which our foremost and best-known members were identified.

The public would not know that ; I have always meant to put that right, correct the perspective, so far as I can.

The veracity of this account may be vouched for by the fact that it rests in part upon diaries kept at the time. I am well aware that the personal approach may be displeasing to some ; but the personal approach is the whole point of the account. I am not writing history, I am offering evidence to the historians. An American historian concerned with this period and subject has urged on me that Americans, even scholars in this field, are without inside information upon it and do not realise its importance. His encouragement has decided me to publish.

I have called this essay 'A Contribution to Contemporary History'. It might also be called 'A Study in Political Decline'.

A. L. ROWSE

ALL SOULS COLLEGE, OXFORD
  Independence Day, 1960

APPROACH

It is not my business to defend All Souls College, but there is a widespread idea that the college, as such, had a large part in the fatal policy of appeasement that led to the war. Lord Boothby — with whom I saw eye to eye on this issue at the time, and over other matters since — has several times referred to 'that disastrous dinner-table', as if it were over dinner at All Souls that that policy originated or was planned. Of course it was much discussed in college, and some of the most eminent members of the college had a leading hand in it ; but the overwhelming majority of us were opposed to it — the younger generation of the Fellows practically to a man, most of the middle generation of professors and some seniors. Of the public men and politicians who were Fellows, Leo Amery was consistently opposed to appeasement : throughout the whole of that deplorable decade he was more right than any front-bench figure, even than Churchill with whom he fought side by side in vain. Sir Arthur (now Lord) Salter, though he was a recent recruit to the college from outside, had an equally good record of consistent opposition. There remain Simon and Halifax, and of course Geoffrey Dawson, Editor of *The Times* during the whole period and the most powerful figure of the lot ; these three were in it up to the neck.

This is not the place, nor is there space, to go into the dual nature of the college : one half, the larger, academic ; the other half, the more important, in the outside world.[1] Between the two wars it happened that the policy and the judgment of a venerated Warden, Sir William Anson, bore fruit in a remarkable crop of Fellows who made their mark in public life : Viceroys and Foreign Secretaries, Curzon, Chelmsford, Halifax ; eminent lawyers and cabinet ministers, Simon, Amery, Wilfrid Greene, Somervell, Radcliffe ; bankers and empire-builders, Brand, Dougal Malcolm, Lionel Curtis ; Cosmo Lang, Archbishop of York and then Canterbury, Bishops Henson and Headlam ; the headmasters of Eton and Winchester ; Geoffrey Dawson, one of the half-dozen most influential men in Britain throughout the whole period.[2]

What a galaxy it was! And how much one learnt, as a young man, from such a company of men frequently coming down for the week-ends, or for college meetings, or occasionally during the week. Since I cannot but be severe with some of them, I must say this at the outset: one thing dominated them all — the sense of public duty ; there was nothing they would not do if they were convinced it was their duty. This was the air they breathed ; I never ceased to admire them for it. It always seemed to me characteristic that when old Lang was struck down by a stroke, in the

[1] I have given an account of its nature and constitution in an essay, 'All Souls College', in *The English Past*.

[2] C. W. Brodribb of *The Times* wrote a little skit on this theme, 'Government by Mallardry', the mallard being the totem of the College. I am indebted to the present Warden for lending me a copy of this rare piece.

street, on his way to a meeting of the Trustees of the British Museum, his last words were 'I must get to the station'. One other thing : though I was a young fanatic of the Left, in constant opposition to them in politics, I never received anything but kindness and forbearance from them. For my part I regarded them not merely with admiration, though unflinching disagreement, but with affection ; for nearly all of these men I had a liking, of some of them I was really fond. So there is no personal animus in my reprobation of the course they led us on : 'Their ways I judge and much condemn.'

On the other hand, I have always intended to say what I thought about what those of us went through who protested and argued and urged and warned in vain, until we were driven frantic with anxiety and despair. I find it hard to write about it even now ; one's heart aches at the grief of it all and at what it ended in — inevitably, though so few would see it.

The dominant interest of All Souls was in public affairs : that, rather than literature or the petty business of academic politics, was what all the conversation was about. I suppose it was this that pulled me out of my natural bent for history and literature and drew me towards politics. During the whole of that feverish decade I was a Labour candidate for Parliament and much concerned with what was going on in the Labour Party. Perhaps I can say without cynicism that this was one reason why some of these people — especially Dawson, Simon, Amery and Curtis — always gave me more consideration than I could expect as a junior, of no experience or importance. A significant thing I observe about the

3

diaries and journals I kept all through these years is that they are mostly concerned with my own inner life, not with politics that took up so much of my outer interest and activity. But one could not avoid an intense political concern in the 1930's, even if one had wanted to ; for European affairs were growing increasingly desperate, and one was burdened by the constantly nagging feeling that if we would only take the right line, the course of events might be influenced for good, Hitler held in check, and the war prevented. There *was* a hope then, and it did matter what line we took ; during that last decade this country exercised a leading influence in Europe and still held a position of leadership in the English-speaking world. All that has changed now : the real decisions are made elsewhere. These men I am going to write about, without the least intending it, helped largely to bring that about.

I

We may best begin with *The Times*, which during the whole period exercised an extraordinary political influence. We can base ourselves on *The History of the Times*, written in the office, with which the paper made a notable act of reparation for all the damage it did, though that was beyond repair.

For nearly sixty years *The Times* was edited by one Fellow of All Souls or another : by Buckle from 1884 to 1912, by Dawson from 1912 to 1919 and again from 1922 to 1941. The three years' intermission were occupied by Wickham Steed, brought in by Northcliffe when he quarrelled with Dawson. Dawson filled in those years as Estates Bursar at All Souls, where he was always a prime influence — working Empire-builders like Curtis and Coupland into the college, and T. E. Lawrence : much to the distaste of Warden Pember, a Little Englander friend of Sir Edward Grey, and a close friend of Baldwin, too, from Harrow days. (Vansittart thought Baldwin had a particular weakness for Fellows of All Souls, as he certainly had for Halifax and Dawson.[1]) Steed had an immense knowledge of foreign affairs and an equally clear head about them ; he took his

[1] 'Baldwin liked a Fellow of All Souls better than other fellows.' Lord Vansittart, *The Mist Procession*, 352.

stand on the Treaty of Versailles and on the Anglo-French alliance, and realised that revisionism would only bring about the revival of the German threat to Europe. History would have been somewhat different in this country if he had remained editor of *The Times*.

On Northcliffe's death the controlling interest in the paper was bought by J. J. Astor. The first thing that was done was to dismiss Steed and bring back Dawson. Northcliffe may have died mad, but he sometimes had intuitions of genius. He was one of the few people in 1914 who saw that the war would be a long one ; Dawson was utterly wrong, he doubted if it could last a year. For another, Northcliffe realised that Dawson was 'by instinct a pro-German': he could not help it. Where this came from is difficult to say. Some of it came from his Cecil Rhodes inheritance ; he was deeply and invariably anti-French in prejudice — he had the contempt for the French of all this circle. A very conventional and moral man, regular in his religious observances, he thought them both immoral and weak. Sheer ignorance of Europe was another part of it. He had received his training, like so many of this group, under Milner in South Africa. At Oxford he had read Greats. Without any knowledge of European history, still less of German history, without knowing one word of the language or having the slightest insight into the German mind, he threw all his influence — which was immense — into undermining Versailles and doing the business of the Germans for them.

Worse, on coming back to *The Times*, he took to himself an assistant, Barrington-Ward, who fortified Dawson's empiricism of approach and lack of principle in these matters, with a moral conviction on the wrong side that nothing would shake, neither facts nor evidence, nor common-sense, nor any sympathy with the victims of patent violence, cruelty, every kind of brutality and aggression. The product of a Cornish vicarage (though not a Cornishman) and of Balliol, Barrington-Ward saw the issue in moral terms : 'That the mistake of Versailles had to be paid for by the Allies', says *The Times History*, 'remained one of B.-W.'s deepest convictions'.[1] The conclusion drawn was that nothing that Hitler did, however immoral, was to be resisted. What a reversal of common sense! — morality was on the side of the criminals, offering no sympathy for the victims. *The Times History* itself tells us that it was not 'believed in the office that Germany was secretly evading the stipulations of the Treaty' — which, of course, she was doing all through the Weimar Republic. Hans Jagow agreeably said that the 'war of revenge had been in preparation since 1919'. Even when Hitler came in and the open threat to Europe and ourselves was there for anyone to see, 'the policy of making not merely as many concessions to Nazi-Germany as to Weimar-Germany, but even more, was adopted as a basic principle of foreign policy'. 'For six years,' *i.e.* right up to 1939, 'the paper saw no reason why an action that was justified by ethics and politics before January 1933 should be held to be falsified by the events of the 30th of that month.'

The simple truth that I saw at the time and held to unchangeably throughout the thirties was that, whatever

[1] *The History of the Times, Part II, 1921–48*, 669, 714, 769.

concessions were justifiable to Weimar-Germany, no concessions should ever be made to Hitler. That this was the right line to adhere to all the evidence now proves: hold the ring around Hitler's Germany, and the break will come inside. The generals would certainly have got rid of him if we had not presented him with success after success on a platter. There was no conception of this in the minds of Dawson and Barrington-Ward : indeed they played Hitler's game from the first right up till it ended in war, having no conception that in this country's historic policy of a Grand Alliance lay our only safety. No wonder *The Times History* now says, 'neither *The Times*, nor the revisionists led by Keynes, perceived the risks involved in the application of ethical ideals or moral factors to political realities' [1] — particularly their inapplicability to a régime of such wicked men, who only used them to advance their criminal designs, and laughed at those who were fools enough to ham-string themselves by such scruples. No wonder the *History* concludes that 'Dawson and B.-W. failed to see that Munich was not an agreed settlement' ; that 'neither Baldwin nor Dawson appreciated the fact that the policy of appeasement, without armament, involved the gravest risks to security' ; that 'the degree to which the Editor shared the confidences and intimacies of Ministers led him to connive at Baldwin's subservience to party expediency and his indifference to State security' ; that 'Dawson, like Baldwin's successor, is necessarily involved in the discredit attaching to the inevitable collapse of such a policy, or rather, substitute for policy' ; that 'Dawson and his friends outside the office,

[1] *The History of the Times, Part II, 1921–48,* 767, 823, 824, 832.

8

with no successor to Chirol, Saunders, Steed or Williams inside the office to warn them, propagated their naïvety and confidence among a self-deluded public'.

In truth, Dawson with his lack of principle, and Barrington-Ward with his moralism on the wrong side — both of them good, religious men, strong in their observances — made a fatal combination. I sometimes wonder whether more harm is done in the world by criminals or by good, moral men who lend themselves to their purposes. And it was not for want of warning. I took every opportunity I could of getting at Dawson — and on the whole he was wonderfully patient, very good to me — but without the slightest effect : I was too unimportant. No-one had a more acute sense than Dawson of who was important and who was not. Very understandably, too : there was no doubt of *his* importance, when Prime Ministers, both MacDonald and Baldwin, would discuss the composition of their cabinets with him. Of course, he was fundamentally a politician, rather than a journalist, and so much more powerful than any of them.

I can't understand how Dawson put up with me, gave me more rope than anyone, allowed me to tease him, and teased me in return ; I think he must have liked me, as I certainly liked him, though without abating a jot of my views, my youthful reprobation of his policy. And how much I miss him now and all that group of friends, from college : the place isn't the same without them. I can see him now on a summer day coming into the smoking-room in full Ascot kit, grey topper and tails, chaffing me whether I wouldn't come too. He knew that I would no more think

9

of going to Ascot than I would of going to Lhassa — or, for that matter, Berchtesgaden.

No, it was not for want of warning. He got plenty of that from his own correspondent in Berlin, Ebbutt. So far from attending to it, he doctored his dispatches. Dawson himself wrote, 'I do my utmost, night after night, to keep out of the paper anything that might hurt their suscepti-bilities. . . . I shall be more grateful than I can say for any explanation and guidance, for I have always been convinced that the peace of the world depends more than anything else upon our getting into reasonable relations with Germany.' [1] There was the mistake : there never was any possibility of 'reasonable relations' with Hitler's Germany ; the only end to that policy would have been submission to Hitler's Ger-many, dominant in Europe, and the complete loss of our freedom and independence. John Walter, of the old family of proprietors of *The Times*, warned him time and again. So did Brand, one of his closest friends at All Souls and a trustee of *The Times*. But, fortified by the constant support of the Astors, by Lothian and all the pro-Germans, secure in the close personal friendship of Baldwin, Halifax and Cham-berlain, he was deterred by nothing. Not for nothing was he a Yorkshireman : he had all a Yorkshireman's toughness, thick-skinnedness and obstinacy ; underneath his good manners he was quite impermeable.

He used to tell me of his great respect for the *Yorkshire Post* — he did not care for the *Manchester Guardian*, he was far too much of a party man and a Tory for that — and would call in at Leeds for a talk with Arthur Mann, its editor. See

[1] *The History of the Times, Part II, 1921–48*, 734.

his diary in April 1935, for example : 'To Leeds, where Arthur Mann met me and took me to his office for a half-hour talk about European affairs. I don't think I shook his violent anti-Germanism much. . . .'[1] Arthur Mann, good Tory as he was, was right about Germany — and was offensively snubbed by Neville Chamberlain when he protested against his Munich policy. That, by the way, was characteristic of the group : they, who were so wrong, behaved badly to the people who were right — Chamberlain, for example, to both Eden and Cranborne. To please Hitler, Dawson removed Ebbutt from Berlin : the treatment he got certainly contributed to his breakdown.

As early as 1928 things went wrong at Printing House Square : Harold Williams, who was Foreign Editor and had a real knowledge of European affairs, died. Dawson, who had none, but a great flair for power, decided not to replace him. This was to concentrate all power in his hands, with Barrington-Ward as Assistant. And, of course, *The Times* correspondence columns, which were never more important with these fearful issues going forward and being debated, were consistently and tendentiously edited in the interests of appeasement. Philip Lothian would be put up to try out some further downward step in 'better relations' with Germany ; or some innocent dean, like the Dean of St. Paul's, or some ingenuous scholar, like Edwyn Bevan, or illusionists like Lord Allen of Hurtwood would be given prominent place with their misdirected zeal. George Lansbury, the old pacifist, wanted to go and pray with Hitler for peace ; Dick Sheppard, Dean of Canterbury,

[1] J. E. Wrench, *Geoffrey Dawson and our Times*, 323.

asked permission to go on a prayer-campaign for peace in Hitler's Germany.

Even the war itself was better than all this : it was at least heroic. These people would listen to no sense on the subject while there was yet time. Now that it is all over, their survivors blame it all on the people — meanly, pusillanimously. For if it is true that the people are pretty hopeless about politics, as they are, all the more reason, all the more of an obligation, that they should be given honest leadership in the right direction. This powerful group did lead, but in the wrong direction, and wouldn't take telling from those who were right. Churchill besought them again and again to tell the people the truth, the facts of our unpreparedness, the urgent necessity to rearm, the truth about Germany. 'Tell the truth, tell the truth to the British people,' Churchill urged Baldwin. 'They are a tough people and a robust people. They may be a bit offended at the moment, but if you have told them exactly what is going on, you have insured yourself against complaints and reproaches, which are very unpleasant when they come home on the morrow of some disillusionment.'

But these people would not believe the facts themselves when they were given them — they preferred to lead the country, with continuous electoral success, in their illusions. That is how Baldwin came to mislead Parliament and the country about the rate of German rearmament in the air. It was not for want of the true figures. He was supplied with the true figures by both Vansittart and Churchill independently. German generals risked their lives in giving us the figures in the hope of our restraining Hitler. Not a bit of it :

these people preferred to lap up the facts and arguments laid on for them by Nazi propaganda, to lend themselves — to a degree I did not realise at the time — to Ribbentrop's schemes, clumsy, infantile, obvious as they were.

What could have possessed them ? How to explain their blindness ? That is the problem. There can be no question now that these men were wrong ; but how they could be *so* wrong, in face of everything, and *why* they were so wrong — there is a problem. It is a formidable one, but I shall address myself to it at the end of this book.

II

The period was bespattered with 'turning-points' — Vansittart, in his self-conscious way, notices the characteristic cliché. But, in truth, we were given many chances. There was MacDonald's Geneva Protocol of 1924, which might have made the League effective against aggressors but was turned down by Baldwin's government in 1925. There was the turning-point of 1931, when the other political parties ganged up to keep Labour out of power — for that was its simple meaning. (True, the Labour Party then, on its performance in 1931, showed itself unfit to govern.) There was the danger-signal from Germany when Hitler came to power in 1933 ; another, when we might have stopped him for good and all, with the militarisation of the Rhineland in 1936. *Und so weiter.*

One thing that Amery and I agreed about in our frequent conversations in college was the fundamental dishonesty of the National government : they were dedicated, with vast electoral majorities, to not letting the real issues penetrate through to the electorate. This spirit of evasion and deception held sway until the country woke up and found it was 1940. All this may be read at large in the books about Baldwin and in his speeches ; my view of it is corroborated by Amery, with whom, among these politicians, I talked more than with anyone : he on the extreme Right, I on the Left, for it was the middle-men who ruined us.

Among the personal motives for this coming together in 1931 was the determination, among these second-rate men, to keep out the two men of genius, Lloyd George and Churchill. Naturally they would be uncomfortable bedfellows, for their instincts were all for action. So were Amery's, and this in itself was a sufficient reason for keeping him out. Looking back over it all, I still cannot quite understand why the Tories so deliberately neglected him in the 1930's. I think it was Baldwin, who disliked his push for action, his campaign for Imperial tariffs, and distrusted his judgment. The curious thing is that his judgment, on the fundamental issues, was so much better than theirs.

On one point it was better than Churchill's, and I had it from him in our constant talks. Churchill has always held the view that nothing was easier to prevent than the Second German war : 'the Unnecessary War', he calls it. Amery doubted this, and I think rightly. He said to me that, after the Germans had come so very near to 'bringing it off' the first time, it was only to be expected that they should have another try. I incline to agree with him over this : it makes the argument no better for the pro-Germans, it makes it worse ; for, if that is so, it was no reason for us to have made it easy for them. Anyway, Baldwin and Chamberlain kept both Amery and Churchill out the whole time : too candid and sincere for the one, too right on the fundamental issue of Germany for the other.

But 1931 was a heaven-sent opportunity for another Fellow of All Souls, John Simon. Stafford Cripps once said to me — with the lack of love of one leader at the Bar for another — that Simon had been kicked off the ladder in 1916 (he opposed conscription in the first German war) and was determined that, whatever happened, nothing should ever get him off again. And that was about the length of it : nothing ever did ; at all costs he held on all through everything, Foreign Secretary, Home Secretary (for the second time), Chancellor of the Exchequer, to end up as Lord Chancellor in Churchill's war-time government of 1940–45. The clue to Simon was once suggested to me by one of the most perceptive of my friends in college, a great reader of Proust : Simon always remained the head-boy of Fettes, he *had* to get all the prizes. This perception is corroborated by a reading of his own autobiography, *Retrospect*. Another shaft of light was contributed by a somewhat senior friend, a distinguished historian, who commented that, much as he had heard Simon talk, he had never heard a single original reflection from his lips. There was truth in that, too.

It may be gathered from this that Simon, for all he tried, was no more popular in college than he was at large. Nobody loved him ; the more he tried, the less they loved him. Some people, especially among the lawyers, made quite a thing of disliking him, repeated his notorious *gaffes* and *faux-pas*. For my part, I cannot in my heart say that I disliked Simon. In fact, considering that I did not care for his type, I came nearer to liking him and treating him with respect than almost anyone else in college, certainly among the younger generation, as we then were. Whether in return for this, or from loneliness or some kindness of disposition — he was utterly devoted to the college that was not very good to him — he singled me out for attention, always talked to me and treated me with a measure of confidence. Alas, he could treat no-one with confidence full and entire — small blame to him, but it was not in him. And there was a certain disingenuousness of mind, perhaps unconscious, that went with a great advocate but was too characteristic of these men of 1931. I remember now how he would take me aside to tell me how Neville Chamberlain — whom I detested with every fibre of my being, like all good Labour men — wasn't a reactionary, but how progressive he was in matters of social legislation, etc. How like Simon that was, and how imperceptive! It was the kind of thing that people disliked him for : it offended them when he gave the impression that they didn't know what he was up to.

Anyhow, at the end he rewarded me with a great mark of confidence : loving All Souls as he did he very much wanted me to become Warden of the college, a thing I had never in all those years dreamed of. Perhaps this may be set down as another mark of his bad judgment, for it would never have suited my book, nor was it what I wished at heart: it would have been an utter frittering away of life and time, when there was little enough left of either. I was perfectly clear in my own mind about that at the time, though loyalty to the college and to my friends made it impossible to say so — there were others, of course, not sympathetic enough to see that, and there would be no point in telling them. But that this was John Simon's last wish for the institution he so much loved revealed a touching confidence.

In return, I will confess that I did his record as Foreign Secretary one grave injustice, along with everyone else. We on the Left all thought he was to blame for our non-intervention against the Japanese in their attack on China — the beginning of the overthrow of stability in that post-war world. We now know that nothing on earth would have induced that pacifist Quaker, President Hoover, to intervene in the Far East, nor his Secretary of State, Stimson ; and that all that Stimson effected was to put the blame on Simon. If the isolationist Hoover, as obtuse and self-satisfied as ever, had had the courage and foresight to stop the Japanese then, Nationalist China might not have been irremediably ruined and America not have to face a China given over to Communism today. And indeed, come to that, the fundamental reason for the Second War was the withdrawal of America out of the world-system : that, more than anything, enabled the aggressors to get away with things. Not all the mistakes this country was responsible for in the 1920's and 1930's equalled the one enormous and irreparable mistake America made in contracting out of responsibility.

Having made that amend to John Simon's shade, I am not going to acquit him of the worst part of his record. That was not when he was Foreign Secretary — things had not reached such a pass then — but in the later thirties, when he formed one of Chamberlain's inner-circle that forced unspeakable humiliations not only upon the Czechs but upon us, in the crazy course of concessions to Hitler from which no persuasion, no inducement, no consideration, no reflection could ever deflect them. Chamberlain, Simon, Halifax, Hoare — the Big Four as Sam Hoare delighted to call them

— they were the men who forced it through, against all opposition, within their own government, or outside. They really thought they were indispensable ; as they looked round they could see no-one fit to take their place — you can read that in their memoirs and their biographies, especially that of the self-satisfied Chamberlain.[1] And that when they were leading us straight to disaster and within an ace of destruction! When before their eyes, or waiting in the wings, were better men unused, kept out — the men who saved us in 1940 when it was nearly too late.

What was characteristic of this inner group, especially of Chamberlain, Simon and Hoare, but of the egregious Runciman, Kingsley Wood and Ernest Brown too — the Chamberlainites as such ? There were several things that united them. They were 'men of peace', *i.e.* no use for confronting force, or guile, or wickedness. That they did not know what they were dealing with is the most charitable explanation of their failure ; but they might at least have taken the trouble to inform themselves. There were plenty of people to tell them, but they would not listen. They all shared a Nonconformist origin, and its characteristic self-righteousness — all the more intolerable in the palpably wrong. These things are more important than people realise ; to the historian they are significant elements. One way or another they had none of the old 18th-century aristocracy's guts — they were middle-class men with pacifist backgrounds and no knowledge of Europe, its history or its languages, or of diplomacy,

[1] Cf. Chamberlain in May 1938, 'Although I know the danger of thinking that one is indispensable, I do not see anyone to hand over to without undermining confidence'. Keith Feiling, *The Life of Neville Chamberlain*, 349.

let alone of strategy or war. Of the most ennobled of them, also middle-class on his paternal side, Churchill has a verbal comment : 'Grovel, grovel, grovel! First grovel to the Indians, then grovel to the Germans ; next grovel to the Americans, then it's grovel to the Russians.' The plain truth is that their deepest instinct was defeatist, their highest wisdom surrender.

Simon had already given evidence of his near-pacifism in 1914. Before he left the Foreign Office he had accepted the Anglo-German Naval agreement pressed upon him by the Admiralty ; but Hoare, on taking over, rushed to carry it through. It was dangerous nonsense. Nonsense, because Hitler had not the slightest intention of abiding by the restrictions it promised ; and what was the purpose of the Germans building warships and submarines anyway ? Were they for use against the moon, or anybody but ourselves ? Dangerous, because it was intended to drive a wedge between us and France, and it did. But if France regarded it with distrust and anger, so did Italy : it was the first step taken to drive Italy into Hitler's arms. Vansittart, so much more strategically minded, utterly right about the Germans all along, but increasingly disregarded, was sure that Hitler would not risk a war until he had got Italy in his pocket.

The second step that drove Mussolini finally into Hitler's grip — where he had not in the least intended to end up — was over Abyssinia. When Mussolini made his move, it might have been expected that Baldwin and his friends would make a mess, but not such a very shocking mess. Only two courses were possible : either (a) to come to terms with Italy to keep her in the balance against Germany now becoming a threat to everybody including Italy ; or (b) adhere to the League of Nations and push Mussolini over — it would not have been difficult, and there would have come into existence a dependable régime sympathetic to England and France, perhaps headed by Grandi, the most intelligent and moderate of the men around Mussolini.

Everybody knows the tragic muddle we made, pursuing neither course, half-attempting both. No point in recounting the humiliations we went through here ; the only point is that we went through them for *electoral* reasons at home, and Baldwin secured another immense trick-victory at the expense of his country's safety. You do not need to take my *ex-parte* view of the matter : here is Amery's. 'Neville Chamberlain whom I saw was frankly cynical. His whole view, like Sam's [Hoare], was that we were bound to try out the League of Nations (in which he does not himself believe very much) for political reasons at home, and that there was no question of our going beyond the mildest of economic sanctions such as an embargo on the purchase of Italian goods or the sale of munitions to Italy.' [1] In a public speech Chamberlain rebuked Amery scathingly for insufficient attachment to principle. Upon this Amery comments, 'After the frank cynicism of his talk to me only a few days before I thought the unctuous rectitude of this effort a bit thick'.

Baldwin shared this limited and two-faced outlook. When Amery led a deputation to him suggesting effective steps, such as the closing of the Suez Canal, or an effective blockade, 'it seemed evident that the whole thing figured in

[1] L. S. Amery, *My Political Life*, III. 174–5.

his mind as a useful aid to the General Election, and that he had no idea of its repercussions outside'.[1] But the old past-master at electoral dope surpassed himself. He secured an overwhelming victory for the Tory party all right. Amery wrote : 'From the electioneering point of view nothing could have been more adroit than the government's tactics. . . . There was something for everybody. My Sparkbrook voters were grateful to me for my part in insisting that there should be no war ; Neville Chamberlain's next door were, apparently, no less appreciative of his high moral stand for the Covenant.' Once again, and for the last time, Birmingham returned all twelve seats Tory.

How did this look to a young Fellow of All Souls who, ravaged alike by duodenal ulcer and acute anxiety, electioneering all day and sick all night, had to go through it ?

I had been at the Brighton Conference, dominated by Ernest Bevin, who enforced upon us that, in the emergency we were in, effective sanctions implied war against Mussolini, if necessary. In the interests of the nation's security we accepted that, and after a harsh speech from Bevin against George Lansbury ('trailing his conscience around when we have to bear the responsibility', words thoroughly justified) we threw out Lansbury from the leadership, in the interests of national unity. Stafford Cripps was Deputy Leader. He was not a pacifist, but he warned us that if we fell in behind the government to give them a clear hand in the danger of war, Baldwin would use the opportunity to play a dirty hand and catch us out with an immediate snap-election.

And that is precisely what Baldwin did. Labour came

[1] L. S. Amery, *My Political Life*, III. 176, 180-1.

back only 150 strong, still minus its ablest leaders ; the Tories swept in with over 350 seats, the immovable assembly that supported the men of Munich through thick and thin right up to 1940.

When they talk about Labour 'dividing the nation', as Simon does in his memoirs, this is the background to it. After the trickery of the Red Letter scare in 1924, after the trickery of 1931 repeated in 1935, no decent Labour man would accept anything from these men, even when they were right — as, too little and too late, over armaments. And for the most part they were crassly wrong in the policy they persisted in pursuing. At Brighton the party elected a new Leader, Clem Attlee ; I remember spending most of the evening with him alone — no following, no court — a pretty glum, silent evening in the hotel. I wonder what were his thoughts ? True to form, he did not say, but he seemed surprised, rather apprehensive about it all, and that would be true to his genuine modesty — in that, so unlike a politician.

But there remained the mess to clear up over Abyssinia. What were we to do ?

The growing danger from Germany was so obvious and so alarming that I would not have objected to accommodation with Italy to keep her in the balance against Hitler. But when Hoare tried it, Baldwin threw him over, when he should have backed his Foreign Secretary, in a shameful moralising speech that restored the unspeakable assembly's illusion of self-respect, though not its sense. 'I was not expecting that deeper feeling which was manifested by many of my honourable friends and friends in many parts of the country on what I may call the ground of conscience, and of honour. The moment I am confronted with that I know that something has happened that has appealed to the deepest feelings of our countrymen, that some note has been struck that brings back from them a response from the depths.' [1] Baldwin's 'National' government went forward with the farce of half-applying sanctions — which none of them believed in, except the new Foreign Secretary, Eden. It made a hopeless job for him, Mussolini knowing all the time that we did not mean business, and would never press sanctions, an oil embargo for instance, to the point where they might be effective and where he might be overthrown. He had plenty of sources of information, and this enabled him to defy the League with impunity and pose before his people as a hero on the cheap. That was not the worst of the damage : it completed Italy's alienation and precipitated Mussolini into the Axis at Hitler's mercy, where he had never meant to be.

In the spring of 1937 I was in Rome and had an opportunity of inspecting the damage at close quarters, for I was taken up by Mussolini's celebrated, but discarded, mistress, Margarita Sarfatti. (I still possess inscribed copies of her life of the Duce, *Dux*, and her Poems ; but that is no part of my story.) The Sarfatti was an intelligent Jewess, who spoke English well and was Anglo-French in her inclinations, not at all pro-German ; nor had Mussolini ever been and she had been his comrade from early Socialist days together. Now she had been ousted, partly by Edda, Mussolini's daughter, who was jealous of her influence with her father

[1] Hansard, *Parliamentary Debates*. H. C. 5S. 307, 2034-5.

and was bitterly anti-English, because she considered she had been snubbed in London : she was a disastrous influence in leading her father into Hitler's clutches. The Sarfatti — she was really rather a nice woman, in so far as such people can be — still retained some contact with Mussolini and wanted to get me an interview with him. I refused. I did not think it worth my while as a Labour candidate, and thereby missed an experience. I contented myself with hearing him speak from his balcony in the Palazzo Venezia. While I waited, ensconced in a doorway in the Piazza, I read Machiavelli's *The Prince*, and observed the crowd. By and by he came out : a short stocky butcher, with a heavy ill-shaven jowl. He spoke with the hoarse voice of a Lansbury, the vocal chords worn with much out-door speaking ; but what struck me was the beauty of this ugly customer's gestures — there *was* something of the artist in him, of the artistry of his people. His people applauded with a conditional enthusiasm : *Evviva Mussolini! Viva il Duce!* They cried, and then turned round with a sceptical smile. I recognised the combination, in this old people, of childishness with scepticism. The same people who were applauding now, with no real conviction, would kick his corpse were he overthrown ; and so it came to pass. No, these people were no danger ; the real danger was elsewhere, with serious-minded, *ernst* convinced thugs.

Meanwhile in England, and in college, the debate continued. An unspoken assumption in the government's mind, in all these people's minds — one that ham-strung any effective action — was let out by Simon in argument with Coupland. Reggie Coupland had been brought over to

Empire studies by Lionel Curtis, who regarded himself as Coupland's creator, as in a sense he was. The Empire-group, Milner's young men, had had Coupland made Beit Professor of Imperial History and got him elected a Fellow — not at all to Warden Pember's liking. But the Empire-builders were right about their man : Coupland made a first-class professor, he was an able historian and accomplished writer, building up a better body of written work than most pro-fessors in Oxford, he did a pile of work all round the Empire on Royal Commissions, and so forth. Not yet estimated at his true worth, he was under-estimated at Oxford by people much inferior to him, so far as their work was concerned. He was no Tory, but a devoted Liberal ; and in all this degraded period he had a hundred per cent record on the right side. Though a friend and colleague of Dawson, Lothian and the pro-German circle, Coupland was never for a moment wrong on the one issue that mattered more than any other, on which our very lives depended.

The government, throwing over Hoare against its better convictions, to recover ground with a deluded electorate it despised but would not lead, had committed the country to half-measures, quarter-measures, against Mussolini. When Coupland asked Simon why we couldn't have an accident, sink a ship in the Suez Canal — which would have blocked Mussolini's communications with Abyssinia and cut off his army there, the reply was, 'We couldn't do that : it would mean that Mussolini would fall!' That was what was at the back of their minds—the anti-Red theme that confused their minds when they should have been thinking in terms of their country's interests and safety. I do not blame them for being anti-Red — the Reds were no friends of theirs ; but we must blame them for being anti-Red to the extent of jeopardising the safety of their country.

It was something of a surprise to me to see how far Dawson was prepared to go in support of Abyssinia and against the Italians, knowing how little he thought of the League of Nations. His famous *Times* leader, 'A Corridor for Camels', had a good deal to do with killing the Hoare proposals ; and when Vansittart had advised Baldwin, in a panic, to take the Press into his confidence, all he did was to call in Dawson. *The Times History* tells us that *The Times*, or rather Dawson, went on being anti-Italian for the next two years. And shortly I came to understand why. Dawson was an Imperialist — nothing wrong in that — and Italian expansion in Africa, consciously or unconsciously, touched that nerve ; so that he minded about this quite disproportionately, compared with the German danger, which was now all that mattered. Of course, there was also the usual contempt for the Italians : no contempt for the Germans — so much more powerful, and Dawson had such a nose for power. And yet the truth about the Germans was stated unanswerably by Vansittart, whom Dawson opposed all the time and even campaigned against : 'It is wrong to regard a nation with unalterable suspicion, but what if that nation gives unalterable cause ?'

On all this I had the most pointed, not heated, discussion with Dawson that I ever had. We were walking down the tow-path towards Iffley — the day may be dated because there was some Japanese prince visiting Oxford. I said, 'Look, can't you let up on your campaign against the

Italians ? It isn't *they* who are the danger. It is the Germans who are so powerful as to threaten all the rest of us together.' Dawson replied with something that utterly staggered me : 'To take your argument on its own valuation — mind you, I'm not saying that I agree with it — but if the Germans are so powerful as you say, *oughtn't we to go in with them ?*'

I was so astonished I could hardly believe my ears. There was no conception here of the age-long principle of the Grand Alliance that had governed British policy through the centuries and with such success ; no idea that we had always made ourselves the linchpin of every coalition against the aggressor who was powerful enough to threaten everybody else's existence — Philip II of Spain, the France of Louis XIV and Napoleon, the Germany of the Kaiser and now Hitler's ; no notion that in keeping the balance on our side was our only hope of safety. The sheer ignorance of it! — but then Dawson, unlike Steed, had never read any European history, or English history either ; he knew precious little about Bismarck or, for that matter, about Pitt, and evidently nothing about what the policy of the Grand Alliance had done for this country.

But I didn't fail to tell him 'I told you so', when the time came. One day, in 1939, when the results of their activities had come home to roost and we were faced with Germany's revived power in all its brute force and had not an ally that we could rely on, Dawson was coming into college and stopped to talk on the pavement in the High. I took the opportunity of reminding him what he had said about Germany, and oughtn't we to throw in our lot with her ? I was again flabbergasted by his reply. 'I can never have said it,' he replied. It took my breath away at the time ; but I do not doubt that it had completely gone out of his mind.

I never pursued him after this with any more arguments or I-told-you-so's. Indeed, in these last years, with his world of illusion in ruins, with *The Times* office bombed by those with whom he had sought 'better understanding' so long and so doggedly, sticking to his job night after night with all the courage in which he was not wanting, he was like a man who had lost his way. As, in a sense, he had — and the country with him.

III

BUT we have gone ahead of our story : we are really no
further on than Hitler's getting firmly into the saddle, and
buying the support of the German Army, with the ghastly
blood-bath of 30 June 1934 : the Night of the Long Knives,
when he personally saw to the murders of his friend Roehm
and his followers, while Göring attended to the many murders in Berlin, including those of the ex-Chancellor Schlei-
cher and his wife. Altogether some hundreds of former
supporters and potential opponents were murdered. *The
Times* did not condemn these appalling events ; on the
contrary, it approved one aspect of them : 'Herr Hitler,
whatever one may think of his methods, is genuinely trying
to transform revolutionary fervour into moderate and constructive effort and to impose a high standard on National-
Socialist officials'.[1] In fact, the blood-bath of 30 June
precisely revealed the true nature of Hitler's Germany :
if this was what they could do to their comrades, think what
they would do to their enemies, and did!

I understood this in my bones. After all, I wasn't a
conventional middle-class Englishman, too decent to imagine
there were such people in the world. I knew Germany, and
the long record of murders already perpetrated by the

[1] *History*, 718.

officers' Frei Korps on leaders both of the Left and Centre : Erzberger, the Catholic leader who signed the Treaty of Versailles, Walther Rathenau, who saved Germany economically in 1917, Rosa Luxemburg and Karl Liebknecht were only a few of those done to death. I remembered Goethe : 'There is no man so dangerous as the disillusioned idealist'. I had read *Mein Kampf*, indispensable to understanding Hitler and the upsurge of irremediable evil he elicited and directed. Not one of these people in England was capable of reading *Mein Kampf* or did, or would listen to those who could tell them. Not only Vansittart was telling them the whole time ; Namier was telling them, another who was entirely right about it all, a veritable Churchill among historians. I knew enough about the psychology of Hitler to know that there was nothing he would not do : he would stop at nothing in this world, however evil. Why should he ? He was the very genius of evil.

When the news of the blood-bath came through, a Liberal summer-school was meeting in Oxford. I remember a gathering of now extinct grandees in the smoking-room at All Souls — Herbert Fisher, Herbert Samuel, Curtis — at which Philip Kerr, later Lord Lothian, burst out with emotional conviction : 'We can't have any dealings with these people : they are nothing but a lot of gunmen.' Philip was a regular Prince Charming : we all liked him. At this time he was secretary of the Rhodes Trust, and the closest associate of Dawson and Curtis, so that he was frequently at All Souls. I for one was always glad to see him. He was fun to talk to, for he was lively and full of ideas ; he passed, in a way, for the intellectual among the group. But there was a volatile element in Philip Kerr, an element of instability. His progress from the family Catholicism via agnosticism to Christian Science did not say much for his intellectual judgment ; and it led him to death in the Washington Embassy, without a doctor to attend him. He was a gifted and generous man ; he was an immense success as Ambassador to America, and did something there to retrieve the damage he had done at home. His friend Curtis said to me, 'Philip died in the knowledge that he had been wrong'. Nice of him, and candid, to admit it ; some of them never have.[1]

For, within a year from his outburst to us, he was off to Germany hobnobbing with Hitler ; and from that moment he became the outstanding propagandist of 'better understanding' with Hitler, and more dangerous than most, because of his charm, his contacts and friendships at the top of English political society — he belonged to the inner-circle — and because of his ability to write, such as not all of them had. I did not know at the time that he had been at the footstool, though I might have guessed it from the campaign let loose in *The Times* in February 1935. (I used to say that if I were away from All Souls for a fortnight I ceased to be able to interpret the news in the paper.) It began with two turn-over articles on Germany and France, 'ardently philo-German', as *The Times History* describes them. They recommended to us 'an emphatic declaration of Herr Hitler himself. . . . He has said explicitly to me, as he has also said publicly, that what Germany wants is equality, not war ; that she is prepared absolutely to renounce war ; that he has

[1] I think I should record my opinion that the official biography of Lothian by Sir J. R. M. Butler is quite inadequate on all this.

signed a treaty with Poland removing by far the most dangerous and bitter element of the Treaty of Versailles — the corridor — from the region of war for ten years . . . and finally, and most vital, that he will pledge Germany not to interfere in his beloved Austria by force. . . . He will sign pacts of non-aggression with all Germany's neighbours, to prove the sincerity of his desire for peace, and in armaments he asks no more than "equality" for Germany. . . .'[1] And all the rest of the regular gramophone record he turned on for them over and over again.

This was the kind of thing we had to listen to, day in, day out, from these people. Only with the greatest difficulty could one get a word in, effectively, to answer it, and then, of course, no notice was taken. No notice was taken of Churchill — none whatever ; nor of Amery, nor of Vansittart, nor in time to come of Eden or Cranborne (now Lord Salisbury). So perhaps I should not complain that no notice was taken of what I said. But, in truth, to hear the exact contrary of sense ground out day by day and to have it accepted for wisdom drove one frantic, as it drove Vansittart frantic ; then, of course, one was 'hysterical', and less notice was taken of one's warnings even than before. A fortnight later, Philip Kerr followed up with a letter urging the reasonableness of Germany's desire for equality in armaments, and this was backed with a leader committing *The Times* in support — widely regarded abroad, and not without reason, as expressing government opinion. Next morning, prominence was given to a letter from another of the sympathisers, Sir Arnold Wilson, M.P. : 'We may today

[1] *The History of the Times, Part II, 1921-48,* 720.

be nearer peace, because we are nearer justice than for many years'.[1] Why couldn't he see that Hitler didn't care a rap for justice, it was power that he wanted ? that the demand for 'equality' was just tactics while he built up a crushing superiority ? that they were all playing Hitler's game ? Arnold Wilson also died in the knowledge that he had been wrong : he was shot down early in the R.A.F. Perhaps if he, and others like him, had been right, he need not have died. Nor the thirty million others who paid the price in the Second German War.

I was not going to let Lothian off; I always liked him, and was not afraid to be candid with him. Two or three years later, when the true meaning of their advocacy for Germany's 'equality' had become evident in a vastly superior German air-force, I happened to have been placed beside Philip at one of Lionel Curtis's luncheons in the common-room. I reminded him what he had said at the time of the murders of 30 June 1934, about no dealings with gunmen. 'Oh, did I ?' he said blithely. 'Yes, you did say just that,' I said. 'Well,' he replied, 'yes. Göering *is* a gunman ; and you can deal with him if you have a gun in your pocket, and he knows you've a gun in your pocket. With Hitler you can't.' I did not press him any further. The distinction he made, on the spur of the moment, does not seem to have made the slightest difference to the campaign he carried on to the very end.

It was at this time that the odious Ribbentrop arrived in England as the special emissary of his master for disarmament questions. (The master was not without a malign sense of

[1] *The History of the Times, Part II, 1921-48,* 721.

humour.) It soon became evident that his real purpose was to burrow into English society and seduce the gullible into becoming Hitler's stool-pigeons. It seems unbelievable now that such a type should have had such success, and still more incredible the people who lent themselves to it. Only Saki could do justice to the theme : it is the world of *When William Came*.

And here is the place to consider the case of Tom Jones — T. J. as we all called him. He was not a Fellow of All Souls, so we are not responsible for him ; but he was constantly in and out of the place. A former secretary to both Lloyd George and Baldwin, he wrote their speeches and remained on intimate terms with Baldwin, was an old friend of both Warden Adams and Lionel Curtis, Secretary of the Pilgrim Trust, for which he did noble work. For T. J. too was a man of ideas ; he had all the tingling liveliness of the Celt. He was a great busybody and contacts-man. I remember a week's summer-school Lionel and I were made to conduct for him at Coleg Harlech, which I think he founded. If I had known the dirty work he was doing for Ribbentrop I should have been less affable to T. J. on his visits to All Souls. But he had the Celt's intuitive discretion, and never opened up on the subject of appeasement to me ; he was the only one of them who didn't come into the open. I knew he was on that side, but I never knew to what a degree he lent himself to Ribbentrop's purposes until his *Diary with Letters* came out.

In this one can read T. J.'s correspondence with Abraham Flexner, a remarkable and interesting New Yorker : in some ways an American opposite-number to Curtis, for it may be said of them both what Napoleon said, less truthfully, of himself, '*J'avais le goût de la fondation et non de la propriété*'. Quite early in my days in college Flexner spent a couple of terms with us studying the institution, before he went back to found, after its model, the Institute of Advanced Study at Princeton. It is ironical to reflect that where the Victorian reformers wanted to reform All Souls out of existence, the 20th century has seen fit to found, in addition to the Institute at Princeton, two more colleges upon its model at Oxford, Nuffield and St. Antony's. It remains for Cambridge to catch a millionaire and found a Cambridge All Souls — it seems somehow incomplete without.

In 1934 T. J. was assuring Flexner that 'all sorts of people who have met Hitler are convinced that he is a factor for peace'.[1] T. J. was extremely close to Baldwin, so that we learn from him better than anyone what were Baldwin's real sentiments about the events of 1935, Abyssinia and the election, the reconstruction of the government and Churchill. Churchill in his magnanimity thinks that these men of 1931 were not personally opposed to him. He is wrong ; Vansittart had plenty of evidence of that, and he is corroborated by T. J. In May 1935 Garvin was pressing for something more like a real national government and 'the inclusion of L. G. *and* Winston. S. B. (Baldwin) very hostile to the last and was sure the Party would resent taking him in' — as these Tories continued to do, remember, right up to 1939, when the Labour Party virtually forced Churchill on them. T. J. confirms that all through the Abyssinian crisis Baldwin's mind was occupied with electoral considerations, as Amery

[1] Thomas Jones, *A Diary with Letters, 1931–50*, 125, 145, 155.

corroborates. When he had got his immense majority, 'he has only very slowly and with obvious reluctance proclaimed the need for more armaments ; he has avoided all trace of the *Daily Mail*'s lust to arm the nation to the teeth and has also kept clear of Winston's enthusiasm for ships and guns'. This was wisdom, and to Baldwin T. J. incarnated 'the wisdom of the ages'. Baldwin ceased to listen to Vansittart, whose warnings were so uncomfortable and preferred T. J., whose siren voice contributed the more soothing passages to his speeches.

For it must not be overlooked that Baldwin's essential impulses were literary; what he liked was words, and play-ing on them, like the master he was, to enchant a bemused and befuddled people : he had no intention of leading them. In addition, there were the arts and crafts of party-manage-ment and electoral trickery. It fell to a Fellow of All Souls, since he had such a fondness for such, to write his 'official' biography ; but before he came to the end G. M. Young came so to dislike the man that he had some difficulty in finishing the book. Baldwin's younger son then took up his pen to answer Young's biography with *My Father: the True Story*. The sad joke is that it largely bears out Young, though it brings home even more clearly the strangely neurotic man Baldwin was — 'disguised', as Vansittart well says, 'as an open book'. It is Baldwin's son who tells us the great statesman's view of the Anglo-German Naval Agree-ment, that initiated the connivance and started the rot : 'The first real and practical move in disarmament that has been accomplished since the war . . . he regretted that one or two in the House of Commons declared that you could not trust the Germans to keep their word'.[1]

Had he not T. J.'s daily dose of soothing syrup beside him ? In 1936, 'I keep on and on and on preaching against the policy of ostracising Germany, and the duty of resisting Vansittart's pro-French bias'.[2] T. J. knew not a word of German, any more than Lothian did ; neither of them had any more knowledge of Germany, German history or what Germans were like, than Baldwin or Chamberlain had. Yet they all conspired to undermine, and in the end get rid of Vansittart in the Foreign Office, who had a life-long acquaintance with all these matters, as had Eyre Crowe and Carnock before him.

The appeasers preferred to listen to, and use, the opinions of amateurs, and for their information, right up to the very end, they preferred to swallow what was put out for them by Hitler and Ribbentrop rather than to accept the perfectly reliable information of their own advisers — both Rumbold and Phipps, the ambassadors, and our own military attachés in Berlin. Here is Arnold Toynbee, 'returned from an interview with Hitler which lasted one-and-three-quarter hours. He is convinced of his sincerity in desiring peace in Europe and close friendship with England, regarding France as something secondary. . . . I have asked Toynbee to put his impressions down and shall have them typed and handed to S. B. and Eden first thing in the morning.' [3] These people were 'convinced of Hitler's sincerity' until they were throttled black in the face. The skies were soon darkened with such doves of peace coming back from Berlin or

---

[1] A. W. Baldwin, *My Father : the True Story*, 233.
[2] Jones, 175.   [3] *Ibid.* 181.

Berchtesgaden to confuse counsel. This was what we had to put up with for years on end.

Within a few days of the professor's return with this nonsense, Hitler showed what he really meant by the militarisation of the Rhineland in March 1936. For a few days public opinion rocked, and the Tory Party, in complete ascendancy, was genuinely agitated. T. J. : 'In two party meetings of back-benchers last week, the first, addressed by Austen [Chamberlain] and Winston, was on the whole pro-French ; but two or three days later opinion had swung round to a majority of perhaps 5 to 4 for Germany. Part of the opposition to France is influenced by the fear of our being drawn in on the side of Russia. I found Ribbentrop just as much obsessed with the fear of Bolshevism as Hitler is in his public speeches.' [1] He had no idea that Ribbentrop's function was to play his master's gramophone record until he was ready to strike.

The militarisation of the Rhineland was another of those turning-points ; and the episode shows that with any leadership even the Tory Party might have been galvanised into action at that decisive moment. But did they get it? Churchill and Amery and Austen Chamberlain warned; but *The Times* did not even disapprove. Their leader simply concluded that 'the old structure of European peace, one-sided and unbalanced, is nearly in ruins . . . it is the moment, not to despair, but to rebuild'.[2] The Germans knew how to take that ; as for the rebuilders, they went on building and building until they found themselves at Munich.

At the height of the Rhineland crisis Dawson came down

[1] *Ibid.* 185.   [2] *The History of the Times, Part II, 1921-48,* 728.

to All Souls. He said to me — I can see him now standing with his back to the fire in the smoking-room — speaking with real force of conviction (it was the only time I ever heard him urge anything with passion) : 'What has it got to do with us ? It's none of our business, is it ? It's their own back-garden they are walking into.' This was the phrase with which they excused themselves for their connivance : I rather think that they got it from Philip Lothian. Halifax in his memoirs uses it, as they all did : 'To go to war with Germany for walking into their own backyard, which was how the British people saw it . . .'.[1] That phrase is doubly disingenuous ; for, in the first place, it was not how the British people saw it, but how they were told to see it by these men who were there to lead them ; and, secondly, there was no question that we'd have had 'to go to war with Germany' — as Halifax points out in the same paragraph : 'I have little doubt that if we had then told Hitler bluntly to go back, his power for future and larger mischief would have been broken'.

It does not seem a very good specimen of intellectual clarity to put those two contradictory propositions within two sentences of each other. And this was the kind of leadership the country got from these people of the 'National' government : a mixture of confusion within their own minds with a very effective disingenuousness where the people were concerned. I remember sitting in silence at the dinner-table in the common-room, a small party, while Dawson held forth about the wonderful reception Edward (Halifax) had had on some electioneering tour in the election

[1] The Earl of Halifax, *Fulness of Days*, 197.

of 1935, how going down into Bolton, I think it was, the people had surged round, practically drawing his triumphal car. I listened, a smile on my face ; within me, grief and anger raged in my heart, to think that my own people, my own working-class people, could be such idiots! I had been a Labour candidate myself in that trick-election of 1935, as in the equal trickery of 1931, trying in vain to open the eyes of my own people in Cornwall, in my own home-town and countryside. They never would listen, any more than they would listen to Churchill, or anybody else who told them the truth. In all those years, apart from the apparently endless illness, I went through Hell, one way and another ; but it was my duty to do so — and there was always the faint hope that I might be able to exert a little influence on the right side, though at the time I used to think of it as a perpetual making of bricks without straw.

IV

The Times, which would not oppose the militarisation of the Rhineland, was very ready to oppose the Franco-Soviet pact, which might, if carried into effect, have stopped Hitler and kept the peace in Europe. We were doing Hitler's work for him ; the game was more promising than he could ever have hoped. The smooth soothers were at work, nibbling away the heart-strings of the British Empire. Here is T. J. at it, a month after Hitler's Rhineland move. 'I had lunch alone at the Carlton with von Ribbentrop and went over the usual topics between us and Germany. He talks English very well and I'm sure does not want war in the West. He talks of Hitler as a being of quite superior attainments and fundamentally an artist, widely read, passionately devoted to music and pictures. They share the dread of Russia. Communism is the enemy which Germany cannot resist alone and successfully without the help of Great Britain. France is succumbing to the bribery of Moscow ; so is Spain. The Paris press and the French Deputies, a hundred of them, are in the pay of the Bolsheviks, so he assured me,' etc.[1] In short, the gramophone record. One almost sympathises with Hitler and Ribbentrop at having to play it so often for the benefit of their dupes ; but they were tireless,

[1] Jones, 186.

and the dupes never tired of hearing it.[1]

The next stage is not without elements of comedy ; it has plenty of laughing matter, if it had not been also such crying matter. Hitler, the artist — he had some gift as a mimic — must often have split his sides at his stooges' *naïveté*. T. J.'s only importance to Hitler was as a means of getting at Baldwin : it was T. J.'s vanity that prevented him from seeing that, for, apart from his ignorance of Europe, he was an intelligent, if superficial, man. Here is a characteristic Sunday morning at Cliveden in May 1936. One or two Austrian royalties had descended from the air ; 'other notables present include Bob Brand, Arthur Salter, Geoffrey Dawson, to say nothing of, as usual, Lothian and T. J. We are all defeated and depressed and hardly know what next to do — for here we all assume the responsibilities of the Prime Minister and imagine ourselves in his place or in that of the Foreign Secretary. For the talk is never of home but always of foreign problems, apart from the perennial game of re-making the Cabinet. . . . The majority are for going ahead with the Hitler conversations, but Salter talks of "treating with gangsters".[2] I have written today to the P.M. [Baldwin], urging him again, as I did on Thursday last, not to put Germany publicly in the dock and ply her with questions as if she were a criminal. There will be no con-ciliation possible with that method. I wish Phipps were an ambassador of some weight and power.[3] Bob Brand is for

[1] Contrast the far safer and more intelligent principle of Vansittart, 'I have always taken the brutes at their incautious and not their calculated words'. Vansittart, 440.   [2] Jones, 192-3.

[3] Sir Eric Phipps, who succeeded Sir Horace Rumbold as ambassador in Berlin, was faithfully warning the government as to Hitler and the Nazis.

going all out to reach terms with Hitler without breaking with France. A German physician who comes over for a week's visit periodically — Dr. Gerl — is a friend of Hess and he brings the same message, viz., that Hitler does not want war but peace.'

However, what Hitler wanted at the moment was to get T. J. to get Baldwin to go over and see him. For this purpose T. J. was summoned by the Führer to Berlin, 'but owing to the sudden illness and death of his chauffeur he had gone to Munich'.[1] We are not told how Hitler's chauffeur had suddenly fallen ill and died, but in Munich, T. J.'s vanity was subjected to the full battery of the Führer's seduction and charm — no-one ever so plumbed the depths of human weakness and folly, or used it to more purpose — and T. J. returned henceforth an ardent and all-out advocate of Hitler's purposes. He reported at once to Baldwin and to Dawson : 'G. D. is all for collaboration with Germany, but worried over S. B.'s inertia, as we all are'. Week-ending with Baldwin that month T. J. subjected him to pressure. 'Off and on throughout the week-end we talked of foreign affairs. . . . I begged him to realise that there was one big thing more he could do before he went — achieve an understanding with Germany.' Before T. J. left, Baldwin asked him, 'What are we to do ?' ; and T. J. epitomised the substance of his harangues : this amounted to (1) trust Ribbentrop ; (2) 'if it is our policy to get alongside Germany, then the sooner Phipps is transferred elsewhere the better' ; (3) 'Hitler believes in you, and believes that only you in this country can bring about the re-orientation of

[1] Jones, 198, 202, 206-8.

44

England, France and Germany which he desires. He wants to meet you to tell you this face to face. . . . The visit of Halifax or appointment of successor to Phipps should follow at once, the points of the new "alliance" worked out' ; (4) 'Ribbentrop seemed far more inflamed on the subject of "German flesh and blood" in Czechoslovakia than on any other subject' ; (5) 'Ribbentrop was confident that Austria would not prove an insuperable difficulty' ; (6) 'We should not be compromised into undertaking to protect Austria from falling into the lap of Germany'. Nor were we, when the time came.

The obviousness, the *naïveté* of this propaganda must not blind us to its effectiveness with those who sopped it up. Shortly afterwards, Sir Eric Phipps was indeed removed from the Berlin Embassy, to make way for Sir Nevile Henderson, who, sent there to get on with Hitler, made himself into a proponent of the Nazis' purposes. One of the junior Fellows of All Souls, Con O'Neill, resigned from the Berlin embassy as a protest against his policy, and came home to be carpeted by the disingenuous Horace Wilson, Chamberlain's right-hand man, as a civil-servant who expressed opinions as to policy. Horace Wilson, of course, had none!

The campaign was on, 'and if the attempt to secure S. B. failed, the sooner Halifax met the Führer the better'.[1] When Ribbentrop came over, T. J. took him down to Sandwich, the Astors' sea-side residence, 'where, particularly, he would meet a Cabinet minister in the shape of Inskip, now Minister for the Co-ordination of Defence, as well as Lothian and the Astors'. Inskip, an old lawyer whose chief interest in life

[1] *Ibid.* 215.

was that the Prayer Book should not be revised, was Baldwin's answer, with characteristic indifference to the gravity of the situation, to the Tory demand for a Minister of Defence. *The Times History* tells us that both Baldwin and Dawson 'agreed not to bring Churchill in'. T. J. warned Ribbentrop that Inskip's real interest was Church matters and that he would be sure to bring up (as he did) not Nazi armaments, but the Nazi persecution of the Church in Germany. The ex-champagne merchant with his bogus 'von' was quite equal to this humbug. Humbug deserves humbug, and this is what he got. 'Von Ribbentrop tactfully prefaced his defence by saying he knew the Archbishop of Canterbury and George Bell of Chichester, and went on to explain that a new Reformation was proceeding in Germany in the interests of religion. Out of the present confusion a new and better Christian church would emerge.' The regular gramophone record followed.

When all is said, who was the greater fool — Ribbentrop or Inskip ?

When they got back to London, 'von Wussow came to the Pilgrim Trust office and we arranged a short secret code, for communication between us when he returned to Berlin. I rang up Geoffrey Dawson and arranged with Wussow that he should see von Ribbentrop this evening.' [1] At a political research group in June T. J. shocked them all 'by putting strongly the case for alliance with Germany'. Nor did he let up in his pressure on Baldwin, though Eden strongly objected to the meeting with Hitler. When Baldwin wondered whether it was safe to go to Aix for his usual holiday,

[1] Jones, 217, 219, 228, 229.

and whether 'Lucy could find a place for her treatment in Germany, I jumped at this and said a holiday in Germany would do far more good than a Brussels conference, and if he would say the word I would have everything arranged at once'. But Baldwin would not budge from Aix, and a week later, 'I said I hoped he would motor back through the Black Forest, but he was not to be drawn'.

For the moment the Führer had to content himself with a visit from Lloyd George. T. J., not being invited, got Lloyd George to take him, and a famous scene it made. I have heard T. J. act it at All Souls, much later, with great vividness — though it is all described in his book too. The stops were out, no effort spared to seduce the vast vanity of the ageing statesman ; Lloyd George's photograph stood solitary on the Führer's desk, the Führer's expressed admiration for the great man who had defeated Germany in the war — I remember it all. 'Lloyd George, speaking with a tear in his throat, was deeply touched by the personal tribute of the Führer and was proud to hear it paid to him by the greatest German of the age.'[1] I have not forgotten, either, that tear in the throat. No wonder Hitler became a violent megalomaniac ; he always had been one, but in the end he lost all touch with reality. All the same, Lloyd George

[1] *Ibid.* 241 foll. T. J. took no notice of Flexner's reproof from New York. 'Lloyd George simply does not understand Germany and can never understand it through the medium of an interpreter and after a couple of interviews with Hitler . . . I could show him letter upon letter which I almost daily receive from men who are the very salt of the earth and who find existence in Germany almost insupportable. . . . They know of the concentration camps ; they know of the blood purge which horrified us so that Sunday morning at Snick, and they live in the atmosphere of a prison.' *Ibid.* 281.

came back to become one of the most deleterious pro-German propagandists ; out of office, away from a big machine to keep him on the rails, he got completely off them in those last sad years of his titanic life.

They were an interesting party going to the footstool in Germany that summer. Along with Lloyd George went Lord Dawson of Penn, King George V's physician, who was 'struck with the Ambassador's sincerity [Ribbentrop had now been made Ambassador in London : he had proved his worth with these people], with his Bolshevik obsession, and with his unlikeness to the professional diplomat. Through-out the dinner von R. kept harping on Russia and the spread of Communism in Spain, France and China, and the menace to India.' There was also Conwell Evans, 'an old and intimate friend of von Ribbentrop. For a long time he has been working through ['on' would be more correct] Ramsay MacDonald. Lothian had now persuaded him that Ramsay cut no ice.' It was Conwell Evans who had ar-ranged this outing to Canossa. General Swinton was there, T. J.'s old colleague in the Cabinet office, then Professor of Military History at All Souls. Sooner or later everybody fetched up at All Souls in those days — that was the fascina-tion of it. Swinton was a talented but rather indolent man, better known for the stories he wrote under the name Ole-Luk-Oie ; I was rather fond of him. An old soldier who knew Germany and, what was more surprising, knew German, he was taken in by none of this nonsense ; he did not get very close to the Führer, but he described it all to me when they got back. Unfortunately, he was not a heavy-weight — it was the heavy-weights, like Geoffrey Dawson, who were so wrong — so Swinton exerted no influence.

Meanwhile, where was Baldwin? It was the British Prime Minister whom the Führer was pining for. Ribbentrop told T. J. that he 'had found Hitler in tears after the morning ceremony. What were the chances of bringing S. B. over to meet him? I let [Lord] Dawson deal with this, and we tried very patiently to make the Ambassador understand what our Prime Minister is like, and how a democracy differs from a dictatorship.'[1] It is to be hoped that this dried up the Führer's tears. There were always people in the gang ready to console these sensitive souls — people carrying heavier weight than T. J.: Geoffrey Dawson himself, for example. At the time of the Rhineland crisis we find him, from his diary, spending 'an hour with Ribbentrop at the Carlton. He was a good deal upset and made a strong case for Hitler's general attitude. I begged him to take his time and keep negotiations alive.'[2] *The Times* denounced France's alliances, which were the only hope of containing Hitler, while, 'as for Germany, British opinion [*i.e. their* opinion] is determined, in spite of many setbacks [the usual safeguarding clause that signified nothing] to come to grips [the usual cliché] with Herr Hitler's peace-offer',[3] [which was only intended to buy time until he was ready].

Dawson now received a powerful warning from one who knew, Sir Horace Rumbold, one of our ablest diplomats who had been ambassador in Berlin, then retired, — a heavy loss. 'I have rather come to the conclusion that the average Englishman — whilst full of common-sense as regards internal affairs — is often muddle-headed, sloppy and gullible

[1] Jones, 259.   [2] Wrench, 332.   [3] *History*, 730.

when he considers foreign affairs. One often hears such phrases as "the Germans are so like us". Nothing is more untrue. I could quote many points of difference. For one thing Germans have a streak of brutality which is quite absent in the ordinary Englishman. And Germans like, or put up with, things that are repugnant to the average man of this country. My point is, therefore, that we should know the people with whom we propose to deal. Now Hitler has quite consistently applied the principles of *Mein Kampf* in Germany herself. He has now got to apply them in his foreign policy and that's where the trouble is coming. The value to us of an understanding with Germany is not only that it may bring peace and stability in Western Europe but that it may act as a drag on Hitler's adventures in Central and Eastern Europe. Once he embarks on any adventures in those regions war is, to my mind, a dead certainty. The ordinary Englishman does not realise that the German is an inexorable Oliver Twist. Give him something and it is a jumping-off ground for asking for something else. I thought that after Hitler had reoccupied the Rhineland he had admitted that Germany had achieved *Gleichberechtigung* [equality of rights]. But now I read that she has still not got it. Perhaps she will admit that she has it if and when Hitler's dream comes true and Europe is inhabited by a block of 250 million Teutons.'[1]

Nothing could be clearer than that, and Rumbold enclosed a pamphlet setting out Hitler's intentions, 'straight from the horse's mouth', for Dawson's enlightenment. No notice was taken ; nothing of this kind penetrated his thick

[1] Wrench, 334-5.

skin till Printing House Square fell about his ears. Alarms from Germany? His mind was more attuned to alarms from Baldwin about the unsuitability of King Edward VIII. There was the Spanish Civil War that necessitated a great deal of humbug to disguise where the plain interests of the democracies lay. 'In October Geoffrey was present at a small party at All Souls, where two of those present were "all for supplying arms to the Reds in Spain"!'[1] Now this was a shocking suggestion — nothing that Hitler did was. And no doubt I was one of the two, Richard Pares or G. F. Hudson — we younger Fellows were nearly all agreed — the other. It was perfectly plain that Franco was Hitler and Mussolini's man, and support for him was plainly contrary to this country's interests at the time. If it worked out otherwise in the course of the war, that was an accident *they* could hardly claim for design. Our object was to gather together all our friends in Europe strong enough to prevent Hitler having his war.

On the other subject, the issue of Edward VIII's marriage and abdication, I am prepared to admit that *they* were right and we were wrong. Dawson opened up to me about the correspondence he was receiving from abroad, from the United States and the Commonwealth, with an earnestness second only to that with which he had defended Hitler's militarisation of the Rhineland. But it was the very fact that the unfortunate king was being drummed out by Baldwin, Dawson and Lang, and to the accompaniment of the usual humbug and cant that put us on his side. Geoffrey Hudson and I tried to bring what little pressure we could within the

[1] *Ibid.* 335.

Labour Party through Attlee and Dalton, who came down to All Souls at the time. From Dalton's Memoirs it would appear that this was the only activity upon which we engaged in the Labour Party — it is the only mention that my incessant activities merited from that lofty forehead.[1] I will return him whole-hearted approbation for condescension. Of the Labour leaders Hugh Dalton has by far the best record over the fundamental issue of Germany and collective security and the urgent need for rearmament. He knew Germany and the Germans — 'a race of carnivorous sheep', he called them and that wasn't far out ; he knew Europe and what to expect. It did not do him much good inside the Labour Party, which was dedicated to the lunacy of collective security *without* rearming.

Clem Attlee, who achieved such stature later, did not have such a good record in this crucial matter. Perhaps he believed in leading the party from behind. And anyway I recall a thing Amery said to me in college at the time, by way of damping my anguished protests : '*It is no use looking too far ahead in politics*'. I recognised the sickening truth of that, the moment it was uttered. I made the comment that anyway, somewhere in a society, there must be people who make it their business to look ahead. Condemned to futility and frustration, we were for ever making bricks without straw ; the truth of Amery's reflection only rendered the more miserable our rôle of watching the blind and the senseless, the powerful and the important, push smugly downward to a fate that awaited us all — the intelligent

[1] Dalton describes this unimportant episode in full in *The Fateful Years, 1931–45*, 112-13.

along with the fools, the forward-looking along with those who would take no telling.

Anyway, Baldwin and Lang and Dawson were right about Edward VIII, and he went. Far more important, Dalton was right about collective security and rearmament, and he was the first person to take the sensible line about it inside the Labour Party. Later, before and at the time of Munich, when things were visibly desperate, and Churchill was willing to come forward on an all-party basis to back up collective security, I kept urging on Dalton the necessity for something like a Popular Front against the Chamberlain crowd. Come to an understanding with the Liberals, approach Churchill and his group — anything, anything to get rid of the old incubus before it was too late; Dalton gave the answer of fact to my fevered anxiety : 'How many Tories in the House can Winston bring over with him ? Only twenty.' I had to recognise that that was the truth ; and there were 365 Tories in the unforgivable assembly that Baldwin had brought about in 1935. After that, nothing effective could ever be done. Even after Norway, in the debate that brought down Chamberlain, when Amery told him 'Go! in God's name, go!', the old incubus still had a majority of eighty with him. Still holding that majority, he fell ; for, of course, their vast majority in Parliament never represented the situation in the country. By this time the majority was aroused to the country's true interests. It was 1940, and it was too late.

Led away by unextinguished, and inextinguishable, passion — for those years decided the fate of our country — I anticipate my story.

Having disposed, in gentlemanly fashion, of an unsuitable king, Baldwin retired in a cloud of glory, equivocal and confused like everything about him. When he left, T. J. had still not got him to see Hitler. Ribbentrop was still nagging T. J. to bring it about — the biggest feather in his cap Hitler could, to date, hope for. T. J. said to Baldwin, 'Otto Kyllman urged me at dinner at Helen Waddell's to beg you to see the Führer'. S. B. : 'Well, it's not outside the bounds of possibility'.[1] We see that it was not that he was exactly unwilling ; it was simply, as his entourage well understood, his inertia.

Only once did I set eyes on this man who for the best part of two decades was the most powerful man in Britain, who had the trust of the people as it has been given to few politicians in our history, who exploited it to the last limit, and in the end betrayed it. It was in the Codrington Library at All Souls, one day early on in my days there ; I was seated at one of the long tables in the bay working, when Warden Pember in full silvery handsomeness came with his old Harrow friend, the Prime Minister, walking in a leisurely way down the length of that noble room. When they came abreast they looked in my direction, Warden Pember with his usual nervous self-consciousness (the subject of the only unkind remark of Oman's, on his election as Warden, 'a returned empty', *i.e.* from London), Baldwin alert, powerfully-built, countrified. There were the so familiar, so often caricatured features, the sparse, rust-coloured hair parted in the middle : the iron-master, leader of the Tory Party, master of Britain.

[1] Jones, 289.

Many years after, when the war he had done nothing to avert was upon us, he came once more to All Souls, passing through on one of his rare visits to London — it may have been 1940. By then he had experienced the full reversal of fortune ; he sat in his study at Astley, and the post brought him every day scores of letters of abuse, vituperation, reproach, from people who had lost who knows what, some of them everything. A good man and a religious man, he suffered all this with dignity and in silence. But he had read my article devoted to him, at that time, and it did not spare him : why should it ? [1] He said a word in self-defence, which was reported to me, 'Of course, at that time I was holding down a job which I was physically incapable of'. No doubt that was true. But why, then, did he not give it up ?

It is usual nowadays to exculpate Baldwin, to let him off. The only, and the best, consideration that can be urged in his defence has been put to me by a truly great man, G. M. Trevelyan, who was one of those life-long Liberals brought over to the support of Baldwin in the 1930's ; and, with true greatness of mind, he has had the candour to admit that he was wrong. (Lesser men, naturally, not.) Trevelyan has put the point to me that Baldwin, like other men, was good at some things and bad at others. The point is taken. He was good at a number of things ; but the things he was bad at were a matter of life and death, nothing less than the very existence of his country. When a man accepts leadership and is at the head of his country, when he accepts the veneration and trust of millions of his fellow countrymen

[1] 'Reflections on Lord Baldwin', reprinted in *The End of an Epoch*.

and their safety is in his hands, he must also will himself to take that responsibility with profound seriousness. It is not merely a question of living laborious days, doing the home-work, it is something far more important : thinking things out, applying the whole of oneself, with all one's heart, with all one's mind and with all one's strength, to grappling with the fundamental issues upon which the lives committed to one depend. Either that — or get out. Witness, by con-trast, Churchill. Yet they all thought lightly of Churchill : Baldwin was hostile to him, Neville Chamberlain thought that among all his many gifts, 'wisdom and judgment' were wanting. It was 'wisdom' to play Hitler's game, it was 'judgment' to make the way easy for him. *They* ruined their country. T. J., in the intervals of his visits to Hitler, could while away time with Lloyd George giving him ten to one against Winston ever becoming Prime Minister. And indeed he never would have become — the Tory Party would have seen to that — if the disasters of early 1940 had not forced him on them. No, I will abate none of my strictures upon Baldwin, passed upon him when I was a party-man ; as an historian, I have only to say that on the fundamental test, the safety of his country and the lives committed to him, he was tried and found wanting.

V

So Baldwin passed from the scene, and Neville Chamberlain reigned in his stead. He may not have had Baldwin's weakness for Fellows of All Souls, but he was even more dependent on two of them. He wanted Simon to succeed him as Chancellor of the Exchequer ; while, on his breach with Eden — virtually a dismissal — Halifax came to his rescue and became his Foreign Secretary. Hitherto we Labour people had regarded Halifax with favour, for his record in India ; but it was quite another matter when he came to Chamberlain's rescue in the year of Munich — it is doubtful if Chamberlain could have held on his hopeless course without him.

For Chamberlain's course was hopeless from the start. It was at one time the fashion to exonerate him and place more of the blame on Baldwin. But where Baldwin's were sins of omission, Chamberlain's were sins of deliberate commission. He really meant to come to terms with Hitler, to make concession after concession to the man to buy an agreement. Apart from the immorality of coming to terms with a criminal, it was always sheer nonsense ; for no agreement was possible except through submission to Nazi-Germany's domination of Europe and, with her allies and their joint conquests, of the world. Simon devotes a whole chapter in his *Retrospect* to defending Chamberlain and Munich — naturally, for he too was in it up to his neck. It is the poorest performance in advocacy that the famous advocate ever made. 'Here', he says, over Czechoslovakia, 'was an intense strain in the centre of Europe which, if it was not to lead from bad to worse, could only be relieved by a concession.'[1] There, in a sentence, is the whole psychological misconception. It is no use making concessions to a blackmailer, or an aggressor ; he will only ask for more. They were all taken back by Hitler's march on Prague in March 1939, after the swag he had got, with their aid, at Munich in September 1938. But why should they have been surprised ? — as we have seen, they had plenty of faithful warnings all along.[2] And, anyhow, what are political leaders for ? Do we employ them to fall for the enemies of their country, to put across to us the lies they are such fools as to believe ?[3] Not at all : the proper function of political leaders is precisely *not* to be taken in, but to warn us. In fact, we were left without any effective means, with no power whatever, in a hopeless minority, with no organs of opinion at our command, to try and do something of what the

[1] Viscount Simon, *Retrospect*, 241.

[2] Cf. T. J. in 1940, 'Who could in 1934–7 have foreseen Hitler's development ?' Jones, 448. But the people in the best position to know did. Why were they not listened to ? — that is the question.

[3] There is a story of one of the most talented of my contemporaries at Oxford, Robert Byron, who was dining at the Beefsteak Club in London when he heard Dawson making the usual case for Appeasement. White with anger Robert Byron said loudly, 'are you in German pay ?' Dawson got up and left the room and did not come to the Club again. Robert Byron, with all his talents and his promise, was lost in the Mediterranean in February 1941.

government should have been doing. We were all too ineffective, condemned to making bricks without straw. What could we do ?

No general election was in the offing ; the government had a clear run till 1940. It so happened that there was a by-election for one of the university seats : here was an opportunity to bring forward a non-party candidate who might rally behind him the maximum support against the government. In Arthur Salter we had an ideal candidate ; he was not a politician, but a civil servant of long experience at home and at Geneva. He was really a Liberal ; the problem was to get the university Labour Party to back him. Here we were indebted to G. D. H. Cole, who stood down for Salter and nobly marshalled our Labour people behind him. I think Salter also picked up some stray Conservative support. In college we — particularly Geoffrey Hudson and I — turned ourselves into a recruiting station for Salter, helped to put out his publicity and collect support ; and in fact we won a university seat that had been Tory since the days of Gladstone.

Salter made himself very active at once. I remember many meetings in his rooms in college, now mine, where he gathered all kinds of people for common consultation — I don't recall all the shifting members of the group, Layton of the *Economist*, Harold Nicolson, Liddell-Hart. Once I remember his prevailing on Chamberlain's *éminence grise*, Horace Wilson himself, to come down. We did not get much out of him, and I was not at all favourably impressed. Unfortunately I was away when Salter got Churchill down, though the vigour of his language, his condemnation of

Baldwin and the whole course pursued since 1931, echoed round the walls on my return. I do not know whether this was the same occasion when he made a brilliant speech at the Rhodes dinner, and told the Warden of Rhodes after, 'Of course, I know that I have no future as a politician'. If *they* could have kept him out for ever they would have done so.

In Cornwall I did what I could to get a common front going. I had an understanding with Sir Francis Acland, M.P. for North Cornwall, that we would not attack each other in our respective constituencies. Of course the Cornish Liberals wouldn't move, though when Acland died I saw to it that the Labour people did not split the vote in North Cornwall and let the Tory in. We would have done the same thing for Isaac Foot in the by-election at St. Ives, if he had known how to take advantage of his opportunity. Instead, a nondescript Chamberlainite, a 'National' Liberal, got in there.

The Salter candidature seemed to me the best model to follow to get this fatal government defeated in the constituencies ; and actually I did manage to get the right kind of candidate to say that he would stand for a Cambridge university seat when the election came : namely, Sir Ralph Wedgwood. (I should have liked Keynes, but he would have aroused too much opposition to get in.) No, Sir Ralph was the best chance — anything to get these fatal Chamberlainites out. Alas, the election never came ; the war they had brought down upon us, by every concession they made, every move to advance our enemies and depress our friends, was upon us instead.

Salter's work naturally now centred in London, and as danger grew nearer very useful it proved, gathering together people of all parties to promote conservation of supplies before the war came. One sees traces of this in Amery's Memoirs. On the basis of our discussions Salter wrote a book traversing the political situation, the course of policy and the needs called forth. It was to have been called *Appeasement* ; by the time the book was ready, appeasement was visibly in ruins, and it was I, I think, who suggested the new title, *Security*. (Salter's earlier book, *Recovery*, had had a great success ; things were too black now for any mere book to count : we stood on the edge.)

As I write this, the news of Burchardt's death at Oxford (21 December 1958) reminds me of another side to our activity, on which the younger generation were very keen : providing for German academic refugees from Hitler's terror. All Souls certainly did its duty in this respect, as did other Oxford and Cambridge colleges ; and much we were enriched by these new recruits, whom German madness lost to the service of Germany. In particular we recruited the valuable services of Burchardt as economist and statistician, of Grünhut as pioneer in criminology. We supported the eminent lawyer Wolf, who came to adore the college and whose only son was killed (like Sir William Holdsworth's only son, dear Dick Holdsworth), in the R.A.F. Not all our refugees were as satisfactory : one displayed German characteristics rather than Jewish, and kept on asking for more, the more we did for him ; until everything was done for him and, the war approaching, he departed for America. It was of him that Sir Edmund Craster observed with a delightful twinkle, 'He wouldn't take even Yes for an answer'.

I had forgotten that one of these birds of passage in the storm was Chancellor Brüning himself, until I read in T. J., 21 July 1937, 'Dined at All Souls with Adams to meet Dr. Brüning. Lionel Curtis, A. L. Rowse, Pares, Hubert Henderson there. . . . He is able, gentle and refined and might pass for a priest or a professor.' [1] I do recall asking him about the cash Krupps and the armaments-manufacturers had given the Nazi movement, and Brüning replied that when he was Chancellor he had not realised how much. I registered to myself—another Liberal ineffective : it was his business to know. Yes, better fitted to be a professor. Is it any wonder Hitler won against such types ?

All through that decade I found myself tormented by the ineffectiveness of the well-intentioned as against the all-too-effective criminals on the other side. Were the former positively *asking* to be led as lambs to the slaughter ? I hardly knew whether my contempt for these ineffectives, who by their ineffectiveness betrayed the best of causes entrusted to them, equalled my loathing for the brutes bent on wrecking the world. It was a pretty pass between one and the other of them, but that was the dilemma within which we lived.

Another of the birds of passage was Beneš, after Munich, sitting in the same uncomfortable Victorian round chair Brüning had occupied. Now that it was all too late, I asked Beneš if it would not have been better if the Czecho-Slovak state had taken in only half the number of Germans ; it

[1] Jones, 359.

might have been able to deal with a million and a half, it could not be expected to absorb three million Sudeten. He agreed that it had been a mistake.

Chamberlain knew no history ; and according to T. J., he 'told Nancy' [Astor] that from the first 'he meant to be his own Foreign Minister' — knowing nothing whatever of the subject.[1] And he soon showed that he meant business, even if the business turned out bad. Indeed, his whole approach was that of a rather simple-minded business-man. According to what he told Amery, 'he was eager to approach Hitler first on the ground that we were "in face of a rising market and that the longer we delayed the higher will be the terms asked"'.[2] Amery comments with an obvious sense of strategy, 'so far from realising that it was useless to try to come to terms with Hitler until we had restored the balance of power by detaching Mussolini'. Chamberlain had no conception of the elementary necessity of keeping the balance of power on our side ; no conception of the Grand Alliance, or of its being the only way to contain Hitler and keep Europe safe. He was determinedly bent on reaching 'understanding' with Hitler. To this end — as if they hadn't already got all, and rather more than all, the evidence necessary as to its possibility, let alone desirability — it was decided that Halifax should go and explore, once again, the possibility of 'better understanding'.

We know from Halifax's memoirs that he was a devoted hunting man. The appeal of Yorkshire was such that we used to see far less of him in college than any other of the college grandees — even of Archbishop Lang, a particular

[1] *Ibid.* 350.   [2] Amery, 228.

friend of Dawson. As Master of the Middleton Hounds Halifax received an exploratory invitation from Göring to 'shoot foxes' with him, and meet Hitler. It was understood that the sensibilities of Hitler were such that he could not be expected to attend (animal) blood-sports — the blood-bath of 30 June 1934 was another matter. Halifax refers to all this in a curiously low-temperatured way, for a righteous man. Of Göring he wrote in his diary : 'I was immensely entertained at meeting the man. One remembered all the time that he had been concerned with the "clean-up" in Berlin on 30 June 1934, and I wondered how many people he had been responsible for getting killed.' [1]

Conversation with Hitler was a more serious affair.[2] Hitler did not think that an international conference would be a useful step. Indeed he did not believe in international conferences, which achieved nothing. 'The real danger was that of an unsuccessful conference. Let us be content to go slowly. It was the surest way.' Halifax : 'I said that I was quite sure neither the Prime Minister nor the Foreign Secretary would quarrel with his counsels of prudence as to advancing slowly. . . . Indeed the Prime Minister had said to me before I left London that he would be well content to see things move slowly.'

Naturally Hitler did not believe in international conferences. We shall see the importance of that when Roosevelt made his proposal, within the next few months, of a nine-power conference at which the dictators could be asked what their demands were and told whether they could be met ; if not, their game would be revealed to the world.

<hr>

[1] Halifax, 191.   [2] *Ibid.* 186 foll.

That then was the moment to face him with an international conference, putting his demands, and his objectives, on the spot. So far from that, Halifax assured Hitler that as to the 'questions arising out of the Versailles settlement which were capable of causing trouble if they were unwisely handled — Danzig, Austria, Czechoslovakia : on all these matters we were not necessarily concerned to stand for the *status quo* as of today, but we were very much concerned to secure the avoidance of such treatment of them as would be likely to cause trouble'.

When one reads that one wonders whether in all Halifax's long career 'wise' statesmanship has ever consisted in anything other than giving way to demands. It is not so much the giving way, or *what* it is that is given way, so much as avoiding trouble that matters. Hitler can hardly be blamed for thinking, with these people to deal with, that there was no point at which they would stick. Simon says innocently, 'It is surely a remarkable fact, which explains much of what followed, that in spite of all the opportunities Ribbentrop had had while in England to learn something of British character he appears to have remained confident, as Hitler's Foreign Minister, that, to whatever lengths Germany went, Britain would be unwilling to fight'.[1] But considering the trouble all these people took to reassure him, is it surprising ?

It was precisely this spineless concessionism, when faced with blackmailers and murderers, that brought on the war. Every concession made strengthened their position. Everybody can see that now. But need one take much credit for

[1] Simon, 198.

having seen it all along ? It was always plain as a pikestaff. What is difficult to understand was why so many people did not, and would not, see it at the time. That is the real problem.

Mischievous T. J., not content to be out of the picture — though in fact he had been dropped for bigger fish now that he was no longer useful in getting hold of Baldwin — tried to get hold of Halifax before he went over, giving him the 'Memorandum I brought from Berlin to S. B., setting out the Führer's policy, as interpreted by Ribbentrop — which subsequent developments have fully confirmed in Italy and Japan'.[1] Halifax returned to be welcomed by Dawson, who records 'a talk in the House of Lords with Edward, who is, on the whole, well satisfied with his visit'.[2]

I do not know what he had so much to be satisfied about, for there followed a series of events which pointed straight to catastrophe. No doubt Hitler had drawn *his* conclusions from the Halifax visit and inferred that nothing would be put in his way. Even that did not mean that everything need have been done to aid him. But, first, Vansittart was removed from the permanent headship of the Foreign Office. He had earlier that year refused to leave the Foreign Office for the Paris Embassy. Even now he would not go : he was determined to do nothing to aid their fatal plans, but instead to hold on in the Foreign Office hoping against hope to do what little good he could. So — another characteristic piece of humbug from these people — they created a bogus post for him, Chief Diplomatic Adviser to the government, whose advice they never took, and promoted Cadogan to

[1] Jones, 377.   [2] Wrench, 364.

run the Foreign Office in the interest of Chamberlain's disastrous course. At the end of January, Dawson 'went for a pre-arranged talk with the P.M. in Downing Street. He was in excellent form and stood pat on appeasement with Germany — not, he said, getting much constructive help from the F.O.' [1] Eden was still Foreign Secretary : that remained to be regulated in the interests of wise constructiveness, *i.e.* making the way easy for the dictators.

In January Roosevelt made a most important secret approach to Chamberlain, a series of simple strategic steps leading to a world conference, with America and Russia both in, at which the dictators could be faced with the question 'What did they want ?' and the preponderance of world-power would be mobilised against them. It was our last hope ; the time was passing when Hitler and Mussolini could be dealt with by England and France, unnerved and fatally confused by ignorant leadership. And, in any case, what this country needed more than anything in the world was to bring America into the balance : we had witnessed the conjuring up of spectres greater than we could deal with alone. Roosevelt would have faced the dictators with the necessity to declare themselves and their demands before the world — and use the consequences to alert American opinion, even more deeply asleep than ours. He *needed* that conference ; for us it was a life-buoy thrown to a drowning man.

Eden was away from the Foreign Office, and the besotted Chamberlain turned down the President's approach, in the interests of direct dealings with Hitler and Mussolini, which

[1] Wrench, 367.

67

he considered more promising. Of course they were — for Hitler and Mussolini : direct dealings with them alone was precisely what he should have avoided ; all along, the balance should have been held against them — the only way to face them. The Foreign Office was deeply perturbed and summoned Eden back — too late : the chance had not merely been missed ; it had been refused. Churchill's judgment of it, with his strategic sense, is that this was 'the loss of the last chance to save the world from tyranny otherwise than by war', and that Chamberlain's conduct revealed 'an appalling lack of all sense of proportion and even of self-preservation'.[1]

Having made this ruinous rejection, Chamberlain now made a personal approach to Mussolini : 'I did not show my letter to the Foreign Secretary, for I had the feeling that he would object to it.' [2] Mussolini naturally seized the opportunity to bid the old man up indefinitely : I remember feeling at the time that there was no end to that process now, since Mussolini was irrevocably in Hitler's pocket. But Chamberlain was determined to open up conversations with him. And he used the discussions with Grandi, Mussolini's ambassador, to beat down and answer back his own Foreign Secretary for the *beaux yeux* — those fine bulging orbs — of his country's enemy. As Amery says, it presented 'a picture of a Prime Minister using a foreign diplomat in order to confute and discomfit his own Foreign Secretary for which there can be few parallels'.[3] Grandi gives a description of the scene that makes one hot with shame to read it : to think

[1] W. S. Churchill, *The Gathering Storm*, 196-9.
[2] Feiling, 330.   [3] Amery, 233.

of the disingenuous old man putting questions all intended for Grandi to contradict, and so refute the arguments that Eden had put to the British cabinet!

Chamberlain was determined to have his way : when the issue between him and Eden came to the cabinet he made it clear that they had to choose between Eden and him, the Prime Minister. There was nothing for it but for Eden to resign ; he was accompanied by Lord Cranborne, heir to all the Cecils and their hereditary sense of the safety and security of the country. There is a characteristic bit of cant from Simon at this : 'Eden's withdrawal was a grievous blow to us all'.[1] It was not : it was a great relief to Chamberlain ; 'I have won through,' he wrote, 'but it has been only with blood and tears'.[2] A far greater man for a moment lost hope. 'I must confess that my heart sank,' wrote Churchill, 'and for a while the dark waters of despair overwhelmed me. In a long life I have had many ups and downs. During all the war soon to come and in its darkest times I never had any trouble in sleeping. . . . But now on this night of 20 February 1938, and on this occasion only, sleep deserted me. From midnight till dawn I lay on my bed consumed by emotions of sorrow and fear.' [3]

Those of us who understood what it meant were deeply agitated. I remember sitting one Sunday at dinner in hall beside Eric Beckett of the Foreign Office — one of the forgotten Fellows of All Souls who were on the right side all the way along — talking to him, the candles flickering down that long table, about the circumstances in which Eden had been 'bumped off'. 'It isn't only Eden, it's the

---

[1] Simon, 244.   [2] Feiling, 338.   [3] Churchill, 201.

Foreign Office that has been bumped off,' he replied. Beckett was then Assistant Legal Adviser to the Foreign Office — he had been perfectly clear about the issues of collective security from the time of the Geneva Protocol in 1924 onwards ; now already suffering from duodenal ulcer brought on by all the overwork, the anxiety and frustration. In the end, he became a permanent life-long invalid, as much a victim of it all as his colleague, Ralph Wigram, who had died in the Foreign Office that winter, sending a last message: 'Winston has always, always understood, and he is strong and will go on to the end'.

(Not all of us could. I was by this time a pretty helpless invalid myself from duodenal ulcer, and desperately ill ; it took a year or two to recover from the apparently hopeless operations I underwent in this year. The last propulsion I owed to Salter, for I was beyond making up my mind any more, having already undergone two operations, with per-forations and peritonitis twice. If I may be forgiven this personal reference, the only triumph in my life is to have survived at all. Having survived, with one bad relapse during the war, I set myself to work as hard as I knew how : after all, it was all I could do. In earlier years I could not accomplish more, because of this miserable illness which started when I was an undergraduate (I suppose even then from over-anxiety and over-work) ; so I had always with me the sense of 'Time's wingèd chariot hurrying near', and the fear that I might die with what I had it in me to do not done.)

However, the Old Man was apparently indestructible — how we loathed him (and that was not very good for a duodenal ulcer either ; if one hadn't got one already, he was enough to start one off.) Halifax took Eden's place at the Foreign Office. It was obvious that at any moment now Hitler, having secured Mussolini, would march into Austria, and without even a word of protest. *The Times History* tells us that Barrington-Ward's 'views about Germany derived from the moral decision he felt forced to make as to the Versailles Treaty. In principle, B.-W. accepted the German thesis that the Treaty was unjust, and he had believed ever since Versailles that the Anschluss was inevitable.'[1] This man with his 'morality' and his 'principle' would have done less damage if he had been a bad man with more sense : he made no distinction between a decent régime in Germany, to which concessions *might* (with care) have been made, and Hitler, to whom it would provide only jumping-off ground for another aggression.

A leading article in *The Times* at this juncture made Hitler's case for him beforehand. Brand, whose instinctive caution gave him better judgment than any of his friends, was driven to protest. 'Brand is always negative,' was Dawson's only comment. The constructive thing, of course, was to give way. Dawson and B.-W. saw no reason to change their course. 'The policy of *The Times* now became more explicit. It had not been adopted in a mood of hesitation and would not be dropped in the face of criticism.' On 10 March Dawson and B.-W. attended Ribbentrop's farewell reception at the Embassy. Next day Hitler marched into Austria.

Well, was it any wonder ? The man had virtually been

[1] *History*, 739, 740, 741.

given the tip-off that it would be all right. For a moment there was another temporary surge of alarm, which I took advantage of to write another letter to *The Times*, in my pathetic little campaign on my own on behalf of the idea of a Grand Alliance as our only hope of safety. This did not disturb the fatuous T. J. : 'What worries me more than Austria is the Spanish situation and its *sequelae*', he wrote to Dawson. 'I cannot begin to write about it. See Rowse's letter in today's *Times*.'[1] As if Dawson didn't know already that I should take any and every occasion to urge the view that we should make no concessions to our enemies, that we should know who our friends were and support them — their interests were ours, that we should come to terms with Russia before it was too late.

Seven months before, in August 1937, I had initiated a *Times* correspondence on this theme,[2] the whole argument of which was that 'the real safety and security of this country has lain in the fact that our legitimate interests coincided with the interests, and very often the independence, of the great number of European countries', and that that had been 'the sheet-anchor of this country's foreign policy for centuries'. The implication of that was clear enough : a Grand Alliance, which was the kernel of collective security to me, should be the immediate objective of our policy. Lothian, along with other people, replied. 'The course both of common-sense and of democratic progress today is

[1] Jones, 394.
[2] I reprinted some of this correspondence in *The End of an Epoch*, 24 foll.

not that proposed by Mr. Rowse, which leads inevitably towards another world war.' No, he wanted to 'see whether frankness, good will, and a readiness to do justice, from strength and not weakness, cannot find a solution of Europe's problems, both political and economic, without war'. These were mere words — in which Philip Lothian was never wanting ; for there never was any basis on the other side for his 'good will and readiness to do justice'. And, really, he should have known it ; they all ought to have known it ; it wasn't difficult to know : they *refused* to believe it. Lothian went on : 'The real purpose of the Rome-Berlin axis is to break the old League monopoly in favour of the *status quo* as created at Versailles'. It was obvious that the Axis was not going to stop at that : it was aiming at the domination of Europe. Lothian concluded : 'No General Staff today contemplates the possibility of a general war, because of the implications of aerial bombard-ment on industrial power and civilian morale, without the gravest anxiety'. On the contrary, that was precisely the weapon the German General Staff was preparing to use to terrorise Europe.

I do not know what anybody else thought, for I was terribly alone, and nobody much came to my support in the correspondence, which did create attention ; but I felt that in spite of having the big guns against me, and being in a minority as usual (and how I loathed this being perpetually in a minority), the honours of the argument were on my side. It did not appear to me that I had been wrong, against Lothian, Edwyn Bevan or any of them. What was more surprising was that Dawson always allowed me to have

73

my say. And on two occasions I got a word of encouragement from the Foreign Office itself — I never knew from whom.

Hitler's annexation of Austria was visibly against the wishes of the population, two-thirds of whom were either Catholic or Socialist ; and he precipitated the march in order to stop the plebiscite that would have made that clear to the world. The tremendous bullying Schuschnigg had been subjected to by Hitler was pleasantly described by Ribbentrop to Lord Astor, Inskip and T. J., breakfasting with him at the German Embassy 'on the fateful Friday morning' as 'friendly and unforced'.[1] Ribbentrop was the man to believe. He lunched that day with the Prime Minister at Downing Street. Dawson went to the House to hear the P.M. give 'an impressive narrative of events in Austria, but wisely did not commit the country to anything but greater efforts'.[2] 'Wisely' — one sees ; one begins to sicken at a favourite word with these wise men. In *The Times* that morning first place was given to a letter from Lothian advocating discussion with Germany 'on equal terms' ; second place was given to a letter from Amery demanding 'an end of all discussions for a settlement with Germany'. In his autobiography Amery says that Chamberlain's 'one fear was that we should drift into a Franco-Soviet combination against the dictators' — the one combination that might have held them, so that the abscess would have broken within. And this is corroborated by Dawson, who had 'an assignation with the Prime Minister himself. He said he had come clean round from Winston's idea of a Grand

[1] Jones, 395.   [2] Wrench, 369.

Alliance to a policy of diplomatic action and no fresh commitments.'[1]

And thus the road was prepared to Munich, where Chamberlain and the French faced the dictators alone, without seeking any counterpoise from Russia, which might have held the balance in our favour.

[1] Amery, 263.

VI

AMERY says that 'Hitler's unchallenged success in seizing
Austria made it certain that Czechoslovakia was next on the
list'.[1] Amery, unlike his colleagues and friends, was inti-
mately acquainted with Central Europe — from the time
when, as a young correspondent of *The Times* in 1899, he
had had a chance of appreciating 'the intensity of German
envy of our world-wide Empire and the strength of the
determination to displace us'.[2] How *The Times* had
changed, if the times had not, for we still had the Germans
with us. *The Times History* tells us that 'the Editor, in fact,
never had any real objection to the German absorption of
Austria'.[3] As for Barrington-Ward, 'it had been an essential part of B.-W.'s scheme of neutralising Czechoslovakia
that her French and Russian alliances would be got rid of'.
In other words, handing her over defenceless to Hitler's
mercy. It is perfectly obvious that neither Dawson nor
Barrington-Ward had any idea of the first principles of
British foreign policy or the essential conditions of British
security. As *The Times History* says of the years before 1914,
'The paper at that period and in Wickham Steed's time had
regarded an Anglo-French-Russian alignment of policy as
inescapable for Britain, and the Anglo-French Entente an

---

[1] Amery, 259.　　　[2] *Ibid.* 246.　　　[3] *History*, 743, 744.

essential after 1918'. One can only conclude, sadly, that it was a disaster for Britain when Steed was dismissed to make way for Dawson's 'second innings'.

The softening-up process for giving way over Czecho-slovakia was begun in June, with a letter from innocent Dean Matthews, who was unable to see that the Sudeten Germans' 'separation from Czechoslovakia would weaken that country and disturb the balance of power'.[1] This myopic letter was given first place. (Vansittart used to say that 'to tell the truth about Germany in Britain was to put the cat among the stool-pigeons'. That did not endear him to the stupid : insulting to their intelligence to be both right *and* clever. The fellow could not be 'wise'.) A week later the wise Lord Halifax from the Foreign Office disavowed any plan that would involve Britain giving a guarantee to Czecho-slovakia. Again it was pretty plain that they would do Hitler's dirty work for him.

All the same people were shocked when on 7 September 1938 *The Times* came out with Dawson's notorious leader — Amery describes it as 'mischievous' — advocating the cession of the Sudeten areas : at that juncture a plain invita-tion to Hitler to take them. John Walter, of the old *Times* tradition, wrote a formal protest to Dawson : 'I felt that our leader on Czechoslovakia yesterday must have come as a shock to many readers of *The Times*, advocating as it did the cause of the Wolf against the Lamb, on the ground of Justice. No wonder there is rejoicing in Berlin.' [2] He received a pretty disingenuous reply — and Dawson could be pretty disingenuous (like Simon) when he tried. After

[1] *Ibid.* 745.   [2] *Ibid.* 746.

expressing surprise that there was not more criticism of the leader — actually the press rocked with it, 'but personally I think the leader was right. My own impression is that neither Hitler nor Henlein wants a revision of frontiers!' What was the value of Dawson's 'impression' any way? All that we wanted from him was that he should stand for the urgent interests of this country, which were one with the interests of Europe and civilisation. In truth, Hitler wanted not a mere revision of frontiers : he wanted the lot. These people were bent on helping him to it, and nothing could stop them. *The Times History* says that John Walter's 'remonstrance had no effect on their policy' ; and anyway they had all the Astors with them all the time.

The Times History admits the sensation the leader caused in Europe — taken everywhere as evidence of retreat before-hand. The Foreign Office had to put out an assurance that no such cession was contemplated ; but who would believe its assurance now ? Dawson assured B.-W. that Halifax 'does not dissent privately from the suggestion that any solution, even the secession of the German minorities, should be brought into free negotiation at Prague'. More humbug : anyone might know that there could be no free negotiation in these circumstances. The only step that could strengthen our hands in the negotiation would be to call in Russia, and that these people would never do. Dawson's biographer says, 'Geoffrey was certainly influenced too by the thought that Nazi Germany served as a barrier to the spread of Communism in the West'.[1]

This was what was so short-sighted and confused their

[1] Wrench, 376.

minds. The immediate and overwhelming danger to Britain was Hitler's Germany. To call Russia into the balance was the only way to contain him, perhaps overthrow him. Amery noted at the time, 'A really definite declaration from the British and French governments any time in the last three weeks might have saved the situation. German generals have actually risked their lives secretly sending word to us that we should make such a declaration in order to stop Hitler in his wild career.' [1] If a break had come inside Germany, as it still could have been forced by resisting Hitler, it is true that the German Army, the generals and conservative forces would have come out on top. Such a Germany, retaining the decencies of civilisation though conservative and resting on the Army, would have been a strong counterpoise to Russia. It was letting Hitler get away with it, until nothing would stop him except war, that let the Russians into the centre of Europe.

These people had no sense of strategy any more than they had of history. Their very pursuit of peace at any price brought the war down on them. Amery noted of Chamberlain's craven speech at the time, harping on the horror of war 'because of a quarrel in a far-away country between people of whom we know nothing' : 'Poor Neville. He described himself as a man of peace to the inmost of his being, and that he assuredly is. If ever there was an essential civilian, a citizen accustomed to deal with fellow citizens on City Council or in Cabinet, and a man quite incapable of thinking in terms of force, or strategy or diplomacy, it is Neville. If he survives his efforts as a Foreign Minister I

[1] Amery, 275, 279.

wonder how long he can survive as a war leader.'

That summer Arthur Salter took me for a brief trip by car round Wales, feebly recuperating as I was from my operations. We ended up with a memorable day with the Lloyd Georges at Criccieth — the only time I ever met the great man, whom I much admired in spite of his aberration about Hitler. No space to describe the pleasures of that day, bathing on those sands below the house with Megan. All that mattered was that the great man of 1914–18 was an inveterate opponent of Chamberlain. He said to me at dinner that evening, his gold-rimmed pince-nez sparkling with malice and indignation : 'I have had many ministers, some of them good, some of them indifferent. But the only minister who totally and completely failed in his job — that man was Neville Chamberlain.' This referred to the complete failure Chamberlain made of the Ministry of National Service in 1917. Chamberlain, of course, was convinced that it was not his fault, but Lloyd George's ; and came into politics after the war with the settled idea of keeping Lloyd George out of power — and succeeded at least in that.

But the mice were nibbling away at our nerves and at the heart-strings of the Empire. Great play in those days, I remember, was made of Lindbergh, treated as omniscient in air-matters, who was able to assure us that the Russians couldn't fight anyway. Dawson quoted Lindbergh to me : he was made much of by the Cliveden set. The deluded T. J. reports, 'Brand showed me a letter from Lindbergh written last week in which he says that the air power of Germany is greater than that of *all the European nations combined* and that they could not be prevented by us or by

France from laying the great capitals level with the ground'.[1]
He reported to Dawson that he had put 'all that I had been
learning from authoritative people to S. B. and impressed
on him that he, by speaking in the Lords today could save
the country from war. He was for peace at any price.'
Perhaps we hardly needed to be told, after his record, that
he would be. 'That afternoon I borrowed one of the Astor
cars and sent Lindbergh down to Churt to see L. G., so that
he might learn at first hand what an air expert thought of
our chances.'

Considerations on the other side were totally ignored.
Amery tells us that 'the heads of the German Army were
convinced that they could not possibly have faced a war at
that time. General Beck considered it hopeless, as Marshal
von Keitel also declared in his evidence at the Nuremberg
trial.'[2] The group of generals at this time planned Hitler's
arrest ; 'at the same time they sent a succession of envoys,
more particularly a German Conservative leader, Herr von
Kleist, who came over in August "with a rope round his
neck" and saw Vansittart and Churchill to tell them that
the German Army and people were unanimous against war,
but could only stop Hitler if we made our attitude quite
clear'. So far from attaching any importance to such
information, Chamberlain's environment preferred Lindbergh's. 'The only result was to encourage Chamberlain
in his determination to see Hitler personally. This entirely
disorganised the generals' coup, which had actually been
planned for the very day when Chamberlain flew to Berchtesgaden.' The Mayor of Leipzig, Goerdeler, who was to

[1] Jones, 410, 411.   [2] Amery, 288, 289.

have been Chancellor in Hitler's place could only comment 'by refusing to take a small risk Chamberlain has made war inevitable'.

These were the circumstances in which Chamberlain was fool enough to go to the footstool, with nothing to negotiate with, never even considering the only possible counterpoise to bring into the balance. Nothing could be more condemnatory than his friend Amery's summing up of it all. 'Inflexibly dedicated to his self-imposed mission, he ignored the warnings of the Foreign Office, dominated his colleagues, overrode wavering French Ministers, brushing aside their moral compunctions as lacking realism, and, to the last moment, refused to acknowledge failure. It was only in that fixed determination that he could persuade himself, in spite of all evidence to the contrary, that Hitler's pledges were sincere, or shut his eyes to the dishonourable aspect of his treatment of the Czechs or to the worthlessness of the guarantees which he persuaded himself at the time he had secured for their future independence and which he afterwards cynically repudiated. . . . Russia's attitude throughout the crisis was perfectly clear. Litvinov had consistently backed the conception of collective security — in effect an alliance between Russia and the Western Powers to meet the growing danger from Germany. . . . Only sheer infatuation with appeasement at almost any price can explain the cold shouldering of Russian offers of help when things were already on the eve of war.' [1]

But Chamberlain was bent on going. He wrote to his sister, 'Afterwards I heard from Hitler himself, and it was

[1] Amery, 292-3.

confirmed by others who were with him, that he was struck all of a heap, and exclaimed, "I can't possibly let a man of his age come all this way ; I must go to London". Of course, when he considered it further, he saw that wouldn't do, and indeed it would not have suited me, for it would have deprived my coup of much of its dramatic force. But it shows a side of Hitler that would surprise many people in this country.' [1] No wonder Hitler used to call him, so Adam von Trott told me, *der Arschloch*. It was this kind of smug vanity that made us hate him, apart from the mortal danger he was to his country. His biographer, Feiling, can do no better for him than to say, 'simple he was, as his letters show, and obstinately sanguine in that he was bent on finding decency even in dictators'. He reported himself of his first meeting with Hitler, 'I had established a certain confidence, which was my aim, and on my side, in spite of the hardness and ruthlessness I thought I saw in his face, I got the impression that here was a man who could be relied upon when he had given his word'. Vain old fool — his *impression* against all the evidence of perjury, torture, murder, thuggery that had accumulated since 1933, and was there before!

Those of us who understood knew that so far from being 'Peace for our time', Munich made war certain and in the worst possible conditions — minus thirty-five Czech divisions and without an ally, save a France utterly unnerved and divided within. *The Times* thought that Chamberlain had done better than Sir Edward Grey in 1914 ; even Halifax repeats this piece of Tory meanness about the Liberal government of 1914. Apropos of the guarantee to Poland

[1] Feiling, 363, 365, 367.

in 1939 he says, 'There was in that no room for misunder-standing of the British position as there had been in 1914'.[1] All the historian needs to observe is that in 1914, under a Liberal government, this country entered the war with both France and Russia as allies and shortly gained Italy too to our side ; after twenty years of Tory domination and virtually unbroken Tory government — smart they were at elections — this country was on the verge of war with both Germany and Italy, alone save for a France that *we* had broken, only half at our side.

Not only Churchill understood it : 'We have sustained a total and unmitigated defeat and France has suffered even more than we have'. Duff Cooper understood it and re-signed from the government with a gallant fighting speech, properly reported to *The Times* by its Lobby Correspondent. Duff Cooper says, 'Not only did the editor suppress it but he inserted a concoction of his own in which the speech was described as "a damp squib" and headed it "From our Lobby Correspondent"'.[2] At this the Lobby Correspon-dent resigned, 'which was really a great relief', Dawson noted in his diary. The Lobby Correspondent was a man of principle, who felt himself bound to resign from 'a paper which was the first responsible advocate of secession and still has hopes of a genuine friendship with the Nazi régime'.

Dawson found this letter 'pompous'. No wonder Beaverbrook paid tribute to Dawson as a propagandist : 'If there is to be a Propaganda Minister, the greatest propa-gandist in the town is Mr. Geoffrey Dawson, Editor of *The Times*. . . . You may disapprove of his views, but you must

<hr>

[1] Halifax, 208.   [2] Wrench, 380, 387, 388.

acknowledge the adroitness with which they are urged on the public. And, usually, Mr. Dawson wins through. His attitude prevails. Certainly, the popular Press is nothing, in the way of propaganda, when compared with the unpopular newspapers.' And that, unfortunately, was true. In January we find Dawson still at it, editing the reports of his Diplomatic Correspondent, McDonald, who had brought back from the Foreign Office 'some rather over-categorical forecasts of German intentions'. As usual, the Foreign Office was not wrong.

As war drew nearer *The Times* plumped, again wholly mistakenly, for the idea of as limited military commitments on the Continent as possible : in fact, as Amery says, the whole conception of the 'phoney' war was settled in 1938. We were to leave fighting to the French Army, while we concentrated on reducing Germany by blockade! — very much a Birmingham business-man's conception of the war. Brand, with better judgment, protested. At the end of January, Dawson noted 'a more cheerful atmosphere in the City. . . . Not so reassuring was Bob. . . . It was a repetition of the case for a Continental army which he had poured out to me at Eydon, and on many other occasions.' [1] Dawson's biographer states that the many warnings Brand urged in his correspondence 'were fully borne out by events'.

So were those of the Foreign Office.

To do Halifax justice, it seems that his approach to Munich was always more sceptical than that of the other three members of the inner-circle ; he had not wished to become Foreign Secretary, and his attitude towards

[1] Wrench, 388.

Chamberlain's course was pragmatic and contingent, not convinced. On Chamberlain's return from Munich, Halifax had urged him to reconstitute his government, making it truly national if possible, 'bringing in Labour if they would join, and Churchill and Eden'.[1] Nothing was further from that self-sufficient old man's thought : indeed in December he was 'wondering whether he could ever shake down with this "uneasy and disgruntled House" without an election'.[2] And this with that *Chambre introuvable* in which he had a majority of two hundred, this miserable assembly that went on supporting him to the very end!

And here is the place to mention, though not the space to develop, another aspect of Chamberlainism that was intolerable : the way these people who were so wrong were determined to inflict their views upon those who were right, and to make them submit. We have seen that with Dawson and his *Times* Lobby-correspondent. It was the same with the Conservative Central Office and those Tory M.P.s who refused to subscribe to the crazy policy pursued. I knew how they treated their own people through my friendship with Cranborne's brother, Lord David Cecil, during these years : the letter-writing campaign organised against them in their own constituencies, the attempts to bring them to book, force them to subscribe to what they knew was lunacy. This is the place to state that all the Cecils, the whole of the clan, were completely right in the desperate struggle sensible men were forced to wage against the determined folly of the majority. The present Prime Minister, Macmillan, had a hundred per cent good record all through and,

[1] Halifax, 200.   [2] Feiling, 386.

taking his courage in his hands, refused to accept the Whip of his own party. When the war came and Eden and Cranborne had to be taken back, never a word from Chamberlain to welcome them or to say that he had been wrong. Indeed, at this time, in the intervals of conducting the 'phoney' war, he was thinking of another peace-time premiership when the war was over! The inexhaustible vanity of the disastrous old man! The country would have a terrible ordeal to endure before that—in which he, along with a lot of other inferior people, would disappear from the scene.

In March the fruits of Munich became evident with Hitler's march on Prague and obliteration of Czech independence. Only a day or two before Chamberlain had issued a statement, as from the Foreign Office, to say that the situation was so hopeful that disarmament discussions might begin before the end of the year. He noted in his diary that 'all the information I get seems to point in the direction of peace'.[1] He broke out angrily against the Liberals for doubting it, and indeed against anyone who doubted his inspiration. Even Halifax was driven to protest against the public statement, about which he had never been consulted. The ever-unlucky Hoare, however, faithful to his master's voice, was able to assure the country of the hopes of a 'Five Year Peace Plan' ushering in a 'Golden Age of Prosperity'.[2]

The country, and even the House of Commons, was at last thoroughly alarmed. It did not seem that the men of

[1] *Ibid.* 396.
[2] It should be recorded that he was responsible for the silly phrase 'jitter-bugs' applied to those who were rightly anxious for their country.

Munich were. Amery says, 'The Prime Minister's first reaction was, to all outward appearances, one of extraordinary complacency'.[1] Czechoslovakia had ceased to exist : there was no need now to maintain our guarantee of what had been left of her independence at Munich! Simon rejected any idea of a system of mutual agreement with others to defend ourselves. But anxiety mounted : people were no longer in a mood to accept the assurances of these assurance-mongers any longer. Chamberlain was due to speak at Birmingham. Though a Labour man, I happened to be lecturing at the Conservative college at Ashridge, and I remember the anxiety with which we all waited to know whether he was going to lie down under this last of Hitler's aggressions. Something happened to change his mind, and undoubtedly it was the forcible representations of the Foreign Office that the position could be held no longer. Helter-skelter the guarantees were pressed upon Poland and Rumania, that we should come to their defence — again without prior consultation, or concerting our measures, with Russia. Halifax concludes wisely, 'If the event showed that Hitler was not to be restrained, it was better that the nations under threat should stand and fight together than that they should await German attack one by one'.[2] It would have been better wisdom to recognise that that had been true all along.

Dawson, however, would still not recognise it, though as *The Times History* says, 'the paper's policy, followed so earnestly and so consistently for years, was now collapsing'.[3] Still 'to *The Times* the declaration in support of Poland went

<hr/>

[1] Amery, 307, 308.   [2] Halifax, 205.   [3] *History*, 781, 782.

directly against the grain', and Dawson himself wrote a leader whittling down the strength and sincerity of the government's guarantee to Poland. It was not necessary to guarantee Poland's territorial 'integrity', it implied, fore-shadowing another Munich when it came to Hitler's demands for Danzig and Memel. It is hardly surprising that Hitler thought we would not keep our word over Poland. That useful barometer, T. J., records : 'The declaration on Poland has given almost universal satisfaction. I say almost because there was a curious and unexplained leader in *The Times* the morning after which seemed to whittle down its importance. This toning down had been inspired neither by Downing Street nor by the Foreign Office and on the radio last night this was made clear.' [1]

I have a note in my *Nachlass*, among others, of a conversa-tion with Dawson at this moment. 'April 20, at breakfast. Geoffrey Dawson on his way to "snatch" a few days' holiday from *The Times*, hoping that the dictators won't be up to something meanwhile. I carefully explain to him why he is regarded as such a powerful sinister influence by the Left : the man who sold Czechoslovakia. He regards it as very flattering that he should be thought to have so much power. Actually he hardly ever sees the P.M. Takes him all his time getting through the day's work, and same with the P.M. Wonders how he is to get through the day. Hardly sees Edward [Halifax] — only last night for a moment. He regards the new obligations with great dubiety. The pledge to Poland only thing to do at that moment to stop Hitler. But these other pledges . . .! As for

[1] Jones, 431.

Russia, are they likely to be any use to us ? I say, we don't deserve to be helped by them.

   G. D. : What have we done to them ? I can't remember anything that we have done to them. Can you tell me anything ?

   Macartney (C. A.) — plain man, simple and good, takes breath at this, gasps.

'I recognise it for the usual D. technique of brazenness, like his correspondence with me about Cripps. Absolutely shameless : I suggest a few things from our support of intervention against the Bolsheviks onwards.

'Conversation closes with friendly offer of G. D., angling as for some time for me to become leader-writer on *The Times*! Not at any price.'

Joking apart — and Dawson teased me as I liked teasing him, and, much as I disapproved, I never ceased to like him and be intrigued by him — it was true that once or twice he had tried to get me to go on *The Times*. I never for a moment considered it ; my health would never have stood up to it, I didn't want to be a journalist, but to write books, I should no more have survived it than his Lobby Correspondent.

VII

In June, Adam von Trott came over to this country on a double mission, an official one and an unofficial one. His official purpose was to make soundings as to the British attitude towards Germany at this juncture, and the memoranda he wrote were submitted to Hitler. The longer of the two is printed in translation in the British series of German Diplomatic documents.[1] But, in interpreting it, one has to bear in mind that it was intended for Hitler's eye and is written, therefore, with him in view. For von Trott also came on an unofficial mission from the German General Staff, and, as such, he gave friends here reliable and faithful advice such as had been coming from responsible people all along.

T. J. reports the latter.[2] Hitler had decided to turn east and act this summer. No amount of speeches would stop him ; he could only be prevented if it were brought home to him what risks he was running. If the top men of the German Air Force were convinced that British aircraft-production was being stepped up, that would help. Politically 'the only move which he believes might impress the Führer and make him treat Great Britain as a more dangerous

---

[1] *Documents on German Foreign Policy, 1918–45*, Series D. vol. vi, 674-685.   [2] Jones, 436-7.

element would be the establishment of a comprehensive war-time Cabinet now. He personally believes that the British are united and determined, but he says that the contrary is believed by the Führer and his entourage. The unexpected formation of a Coalition government representative of our "war-mongers" and of our Left might convince the German government that we cannot be relied on to remain passive and ineffectual. This he feels *might* stay their hand.'

This was perfectly sincere advice, and this was the true Adam. I had, by this time, ceased to see him or to talk with him, for I was no longer sure, though for most of that decade he was my most intimate friend and I can only say here that my emotional life was intensely bound up with him. Poor Adam, he came to a most terrible end, thereby vindicating his essential sincerity and truth ; he has now entered into history. I always felt that our intense and unhappy friendship — for Adam, like his people, had a great gift for creating unhappiness among those around him — had a certain symbolic quality about it : there was all the impossibility in it, in spite of our intimacy and affection, of friendship between England and Germany. However, to set against all the unhappiness, this intense friendship gave me a window into the German soul. I intend to write about it some day, for I still have all his letters ; mine to him were destroyed, I believe, in the dangers of his double life in Germany.

We met at All Souls when we were both young, and he came to lunch with General Swinton. I agreed with Claire Siegfried, who thought his the most beautiful head she had ever seen : immensely lofty forehead, deep-violet eyes, nobility and sadness in the expression even when young, infinitely sensitive and understanding. (I think it was that that touched me most : I had never met anything like it.) Terrible to think how he came by his end : that head upon a butcher's meat-hook in Plötzensee prison.

We kept in touch, and shortly the Rhodes Trust opened the ranks again to a certain number of scholars from Germany. Dawson asked me if I was in favour. I would have preferred them from France. Impossible, and anyway contrary to Cecil Rhodes's will. With some misgivings, I was in favour. I recommended Adam for a Rhodes scholarship, and later he came up to Balliol.

Once he came down to Cornwall to stay, and in 1931, that ghastly year, I went to stay in Berlin. His uncle had a flat in the Schloss, the immense Imperial Palace of the Kaiser : he was a von Schweinitz, whose father had been Bismarck's ambassador to Russia. In the evenings Adam and I used to roam around the Palace. I well recall the Kaiser's study : the telephone cords looking as if they had been just cut, the big desk made of timbers from Nelson's *Victory*, the books half German and half English, half Lutheran theology, half contemporary history and biography. I still recall among them Churchill's biography of his father, Lord Randolph, and Bishop Boyd-Carpenter on *Prayer*. Behind the doors everywhere, I was surprised to see, were stacked pictures of the *Allerhöchste* in peacock attitudes, eagles in his helmet, flunkeys bowing before him — just stacked in the corner waiting for his return.

But it was a more fearful spectre that returned in 1933.

When Hitler came in I knew that that was the end of all our hopes, and warned Adam faithfully to give up politics : nothing more to be done so long as Hitler was there, one might as well roll up the map of Europe. I thought of a wonderful subject of research for Adam to bury himself in : a great book, a parallel to Burckhardt's *Civilisation of the Renaissance in Italy*, only for Germany and the north-western lands, the Netherlands and England.

But Adam could not do it. And here we diverged deeply. He gave himself up to Hegelianism ; it profoundly affected his mind, though his mind must have been inherently disposed to it : for all external appearances, Adam was deeply German. With him black was never black, and white white ; black was always in process of becoming white, white of becoming black. Nothing was clearly defined from anything else ; nothing ultimately was different from anything else ; the boundaries of everything were unclear, nor was there any certainty anywhere in the universe.

This was the constant burden of his letters, and I could not bear it. No doubt it represented the bottomless uncertainty of an upheaved epoch in Germany, a universal *Verschmelzung*. But I had no sympathy whatever with Adam making that the principle of his intellectual life. I loathed Hegelianism — as I still do ; with me black was black and white was white, what was true was true, what was not was untrue. More, I deeply disapproved of this formlessness of mind, in which there was no certainty, nothing definite but might become its opposite. I really regarded it as the intellectual disease it is ; but it is deeply German, profoundly characteristic of their way of thinking.

94

However, I understood it, and that gave me an understanding of the real inwardness of the German mind.

So there was a fundamental disaccord between Adam and me intellectually : he was Hegelian philosopher turning to law and politics, I was poet and historian turned by circumstances to politics.

There was another element in our complex relationship. He got his 'socialism', what there was of it, from me.[1] At the moment Hitler came in, Adam and his young friends were translating my adolescent book, *Politics and the Younger Generation*, in the columns of their *Neue Blätter für den Sozialismus*. More important matters than the translation of my juvenilia were brought to an end thus. There was in Adam a desire to exert an influence on me, if only as so much evidence of his value for me. I could not conceive of myself being influenced by deleterious Hegelian rubbish. It was like England and Germany ; our relations became more and more jarring, in their nature incapable of fulfilment, though, with mutual good feeling, never an ill word passed between us.

On one of Adam's later visits to Oxford, it fell to me to introduce him and Helmuth von Moltke, who was Lionel Curtis's friend.[2] It seems somehow symbolic that those two, who were to die together in July 1944, should have met first in the hall at All Souls by the fireside before dinner. I shall not forget the mutually appraising, slightly suspicious look those two gave each other in the increasing dangers of the

[1] There has been a good deal of discussion in Germany on the subject of Adam's socialism, since his is now an historic name.
[2] *v.* Lionel Curtis' pamphlet, *A German of the Resistance*.

later thirties. Though Helmuth was Lionel's friend, not mine, I could not but regard him as a finer type than Adam — more integrated and in complete control, nearly six feet and a half (Adam was six feet four), dark and glittering, he looked like a sword.

So far as I know, von Moltke had no relations with the evil thing ; he kept himself completely aloof. But Adam entered deeply, ambivalently, into relations with the Nazis, without being one, indeed while belonging to the resistance movement. It was this Hegelianism in action that caught him in the toils in the end. Even though at bottom he was sincere, and his brave end proved it, while this was the situation I did not wish to see him. He would come to All Souls to see Warden Adams ; he was no longer welcome to see me. At a certain point, on both private and public grounds, I decided that the relationship should end. Though I am ashamed to say so, I was not sure that he was not reporting back to Berlin what our opinions and attitudes were.

Such is the background of Adam's last visit on the eve of the war, and of his report to Hitler — on the basis of which he became, while still a member of the resistance, an official in the Nazi Foreign Ministry. (One could not play those games indefinitely with Hitler, and I always thought Adam would make a most ineffective conspirator.) [1]

'Conscious of the present hostility, I first went to stay at an hotel in London, let my acquaintances know by telephone and waited. Lord and Lady Astor, whose son, a fellow

[1] For the continued ambivalence of Adam's attitude, *e.g.* in regard to East and West, *v.* Gerhard Ritter, *The German Resistance*, 263 foll.

student of mine at Oxford [*i.e.* David Astor], I now met again in London, invited me to their country house at Cliveden. There I learned that Lord Halifax, Lord Lothian, Sir Thomas Inskip, and a number of other government politicians had been invited for this week-end — a fortunate coincidence for me. Supported only by my host, who is still as markedly Germanophile as ever, as well as by his like-minded son, I sensed that the general attitude towards me was one of unusual embarrassment.' Adam decided to go over to the attack, putting the German case as persuasively as he knew how. He reports Halifax as replying that 'after the Munich conference he had seen the way open for a new consolidation of powers, in which Germany would have the preponderance in Central and South-East Europe, a "not too unfriendly Spain and Italy" would leave unthreatened British positions in the Mediterranean and the Middle East. After Munich his confidence in the sincerity of Germany's desire for understanding had lessened, and after the occupation of Prague people in Britain had been asking in consternation, "who is going to be attacked next ?" It was only in sheer "self-defence" that he had then adopted the new policy of guarantees and alliances.'

Adam replied with the gramophone record : 'The dwindling of German confidence after Munich was to be attributed to the general and undisguised opposition to this agreement among the British people and to the feverish rearmament psychosis in Britain which immediately succeeded it'. (There was nothing feverish about it : it was all too dilatory.)

Lord Astor, an inherently good man, almost a saint —

there was the trouble, he did not know how evil others could be — remarked that 'he and his friends had, even after Munich, advocated concrete concessions to Germany's right to live. . . . By the occupation of Prague, Germany had deprived her friends in Britain of the weapon which would have enabled them to support us.'

Lothian now took charge of the conversation, in which he made a suggestion of the greatest danger to this country's vital interests. Adam judged that Lothian, though already nominated ambassador to America, 'has not yet gone over to the anti-German, Anglo-American camp'. Lothian conceded the whole case to the Germans — 'the use of force and self-help had represented the only, and therefore legitimate, means for the Germans'. What an argument for a Liberal! 'The only, *and therefore legitimate*, means' — what an argument in logic for an educated man! It was only the destruction of the Czech nation that had obliged him to fall into line with the change in British public opinion.

Adam, for the consumption of the Führer, felt that 'Lord Lothian had an instinctively correct appreciation of the greatness of our Führer. . . . In the circle of Astor, Halifax, Chamberlain, etc., he exercises very strong influence — since he is undoubtedly the cleverest and most supple politician among them.' (He was certainly the most unstable, and the most plausible, among them.) 'In view of his mission to the United States and the present atmosphere there, Lothian obviously wants to avoid the suspicion that he has not yet been converted from his idea of reconciliation with Germany.' So he demanded secrecy for the dangerous suggestion he now made. He accepted completely the necessity for Hitler's strategic elimination of Czechoslovakia. Now, if only Hitler would hand back a measure of national independence, only to Bohemia and Moravia, recognise Czech national identity, nothing would stand in the way of Hitler's leadership in Europe. Certainly Danzig and the Polish question would find an obvious solution in increased economic and geographical dependence on Germany. Such a gesture on the part of the Führer, 'then Europe can no longer deny his claim to leadership, nor can England-America any longer refuse the most far-reaching co-operation'.

Here was the most dangerous suggestion that could possibly have been made. It is ironic that, through von Trott, the German General Staff should have been sending us advice that might have stopped Hitler, while, also through von Trott, Lothian should have sent just the advice that would have enabled Hitler to get away with everything. Fortunately, he was too far gone to take it ; evil men are betrayed by immoderation more than anything. (Bismarck was an evil influence in Europe, but he was a moderate, who knew where to stop.) If Hitler had had the decency to hand back a simulacrum of independence to the Czechs, he would have had the British government eating out of his hand ; he could have got away with Danzig, without opposition ; he would have had Poland at his mercy, and not only Poland, but all Europe.

Lothian betrayed this to von Trott. 'Lord Lothian and his friends are genuinely prepared to concede to Germany this claim and a free hand economically in Eastern Europe, but they believe they cannot do this until, by a demonstrative

99

act, we have restored their position in the eyes of British public opinion.'

There is a great deal more, but nothing equal to this in importance. Adam also saw Chamberlain : 'The Astors have access to him at any time, so that the meeting came about quite naturally'. He got nothing from that quarter but self-justification and reproaches : 'Do you believe that I enter into these obligations gladly ? Herr Hitler forces me to it.' But we do learn Chamberlain's view that 'the small group of Conservatives who are rebelling against him — Eden, Churchill, Duff Cooper — could be completely ignored, and that because of his large majority he need not pay any great attention to the Opposition'.

Adam also saw Garvin, editor of the *Observer*, another Astor paper, and Dawson : 'Mr. Dawson stated that he would gladly receive any constructive suggestion for his Press policy. Both, however, agreed that for the time being it was impossible to advocate actively Germany's cause, without calling forth a storm of indignation.'

There is an unidentified enclosure along with Adam's memorandum, dated from Cliveden. From the language of it, I identify it as Lothian's : it is in the same terms as he used to me.

We have reason to be grateful that German greed and immoderation overreached themselves. If Hitler had listened to Lothian's suggestion, we should today be living (if at all) in a Europe dominated by Germany. If Germany today has lost everything, exists, divided in two between East and West — what a difference from the Germany of 1871, or even of 1918! — it is nobody's fault but her own. A fatal people, fated, as Moeller van den Bruck said, to make trouble for themselves and for everybody else.

Adam one day said to me, 'If they kill me, you will never forgive them, will you ?' This was not a wish expressed, but merely a comment — I thought it presumed a little on my love for him, which was not inexhaustible. My view of the Germans did not rest on him, but on the observation of their behaviour in history, particularly modern history.

But it shows that he must have envisaged his end, and still went on in this Hegelian ambivalence, conspiring to the last.

In *The New Yorker* I read an account of Plötzensee, the scene of his end, and of the annual service of commemoration of those July victims : the inner courtyard turned into a memorial, evergreen bushes in front of the wall carrying their names. Some day I must go, like the American, who, making his way into a dark shed with barred windows, 'saw a heavy cross-beam with six butcher's hooks jutting from it. A few bunches of flowers and small wreaths lay on the ground under the hooks.' [1]

[1] *The New Yorker*, 13 Dec. 1958.

VIII

Even at this late hour it was doubtful whether these men would do what was necessary. From a letter from Brand to Dawson it is clear that he did not trust them to. He wrote, 28 June, 'One hears in various quarters that now that the Government have to face the consequences of their Polish guarantee, they may be hesitating. Heaven knows none of us want a war. But, if we have another Munich, then no-one in the world will follow us, and Europe, East and Central, must all line up with Germany. The Peace Front disappears with appeasement. I heard the P.M. a very short time ago sing a Paean of Praise in honour of Munich as a great success, so he may want another. Surely the only thing they *can* do is to stand up to their guarantee boldly. . . . I do hope *The Times* will take this line. . . . I believe the moment is to the last degree critical and that we ought to form some form of National Government. If that is impossible owing to the P.M., then the Government should be strengthened by bringing in people like Winston, who will make a firm stand and will be known throughout the world to be ready for a firm stand. As at present constituted the Cabinet seems either "career" men or hopeless mugwumps.'[1]

Anyone who knows Brand knows how characteristic

[1] Wrench, 393, 394.

that letter is both in sureness of judgment and in penetrating candour : no cant in this quarter! But his judgment of the so-called 'National Government' was no other than I had been urging all along. Dawson had no intention of taking this line. His diary deplores the *Daily Telegraph* joining 'in the hue and cry for the inclusion of Winston in the Cabinet in order to impress the Germans'. 'July 6. I went down to the House of Commons for a brief talk with the Prime Minister, who was full of vigour, had no intention of being bounced into taking back Winston, didn't hope much of Russia, but thought we should get agreement.' If that was his attitude towards the negotiations with Russia, need we be surprised that the Russians proved him wrong once more ? Dawson found the news of 'an impending Nazi-Soviet Pact' and his friend Ribbentrop 'going to Moscow to sign it . . . somewhat startling'. He regarded it merely as justification of 'the suspicion of Russian good faith which some of us had long held'. No idea how much they were themselves responsible for the situation, nor, even now, that it portended immediate war. It merely made Chamberlain 'rather angry with all foreigners — Hitler and the Bolshies for their duplicity, the French for giving confidential information away'. The old Birmingham business-man — 'looking at world-affairs through the wrong end of the municipal drain-pipe', according to Winston, 'a good Lord Mayor of Birmingham in a lean year', according to L. G., his mind 'tuned in to the Midland Regional', according to Attlee — had insisted on conducting his own foreign policy without any knowledge of foreigners. As Vansittart said, he had no idea what Germans were like.

The Munich set, their policy utterly bankrupt, were now reduced to waiting for something to turn up. They grasped at the slightest straw. Dawson, on 30 August, 'lunched with Waldorf [Astor] at the Ritz to meet Congressman Hamilton Fish. . . . Both Fish (fresh from Berlin) and David [Astor] with his young German contacts were convinced that there would be no war.'[1] The usual bad judgment. The moment I heard of the Nazi-Soviet Pact I drew my own conclusions: I was starting on a tour of Brittany : I packed up and came straight home.

— To listen, on the coast of Cornwall, to the most dismal, flat, uninspiring speech — I could imagine the drooping moustaches — with which any country can ever have been led into a fight for its very existence by its accredited leader. 'Everything that I have worked for, everything that I have hoped for, everything that I have believed in during my public life, has crashed into ruins.'[2] What a spirit ! I remember registering at the time : no notion what day it was to inspire our resolution — 3 September, the day of Oliver Cromwell's great victories of Dunbar and the 'crowning mercy' of Worcester, the day on which that mighty spirit went out in a thunderstorm. All Neville Chamberlain could think about was the crash of the card-castle of his illusions — as if that were what chiefly mattered !

'War wins nothing, cures nothing, ends nothing,' had been the burden of his song all along.[3] Mere pacifist clichés, ignorant and untrue. Unfortunately history has often shown the contrary to be correct. The Napoleonic war and Trafalgar *won* a century of complete and blissful security for

[1] Wrench, 396.   [2] Feiling, 416.   [3] *Ibid.* 404.

this country ; Waterloo *ended* the century-long attempt of France to dominate Europe ; as the war we were just about to enter *ended* the similar attempt of Germany. As for cure, nothing but war could now end Hitler and the Nazis. Really, these people who had been in charge of our destinies throughout that decade, and had led us to this, should not have corrupted themselves and the nation by talking such nonsense.

Naturally, they were no better at conducting the war they had brought down on us in the worst possible conditions, than they had been at conducting the peace. Here Amery's evidence is much to the point — and these people were his friends, though they kept him out because he meant business. 'Loathing war passionately he [Chamberlain] was determined to wage as little of it as possible. (It was not till 5th February that Churchill was asked to attend the Supreme War Council, apparently purely as a listener!) . . . When attention was drawn in Parliament to what the German Air Force were doing to undefended Polish towns and villages Chamberlain and Halifax wagged reproving fingers suggesting the possibility of reprisals. . . . To my consternation he [Kingsley Wood] told me that there was no question of our bombing even the munition works at Essen, which were private property, or lines of communication, and that doing so would alienate American opinion. To my question whether we were not going to lift a finger to help the Poles he had no answer. My diary says that "I went away very angry".' [1]

Our own agony was shortly to come. And to the

[1] Amery, 328, 330.

argument of these people later that they had won time for the nation, Amery answers, 'By March Hitler could claim, without undue boasting, that Germany's fighting power had increased more in the last five months than in the previous seven years. . . . In any case we could have done something to disorganise the German policy of piling up strength for the overwhelming blow at the chosen time and chosen place.' [1] As for the campaign in Norway, 'Our pilots were not even allowed to attack German-held aerodromes in Denmark and Norway till 11th April, and even then, for another two days only allowed to machine-gun, but forbidden to drop bombs! . . . As for the break-through in May, what could have suited the Germans better than to be able to mount that immense operation with the undisturbed use of all their communications by rail, road, canal and river up to the moment when Hitler showed what he thought of the "humanitarian" air-truce by smothering defenceless Rotterdam in flames ?'

No : their settled conception of the 'phoney' war — fighting a war for survival with hands tied behind our backs — was consistent with their policy of appeasement : it was appeasement in war, and it would have lost us the war as they had lost us the peace.

Their time was up. It must have given Amery an intense pleasure to have been the one to give them the order to go — and in Oliver Cromwell's words : 'You have sat too long here for any good you have been doing. Depart, I say, and let us have done with you. In the name of God, go!' [2] Even after that crucial debate, in which the sense of

[1] Amery, 331, 332.   [2] Ibid. 365.

106

the nation at last got through to them, Chamberlain intended to stay on if he could. A fact that Amery himself told me, though it appears neither in his memoirs nor Chamberlain's biography, is that the morning after the debate Chamberlain rang him up, expressing regret that no place had been found for him hitherto, would he now join the government? Amery being the leader of the Conservative malcontents, Chamberlain must have hoped that this would bring them back and enable him to go on.

But only a real and true government of all the nation could do any good. This meant all parties.

The question was, who was to head it?

The Labour Party at last had their revenge on Neville Chamberlain for all the past decade: he was by name excluded.

And here, I confess, I made my mistake. Instinct told me that Churchill was the man, but I did not dare go so far. Chamberlain was still in command of the majority in the House; the Tory Party was behind him. The obvious compromise, reason said, was Halifax. And in that sense I wrote my letter to *The Times*, which, according with Dawson's own sentiments, was given, for the only time in my life, first place in the paper. It has only lately been revealed that the King preferred Halifax, and so apparently did Attlee. So I was in good company, but nevertheless wrong. When it came to the decision among the three of them, Chamberlain being ruled out, Churchill chose himself.

No-one can say that he didn't choose right.

IX

WHILE all this was going on, and the most eminent of our Fellows (in the public eye) so much involved, it may be imagined that life in college had an excitement and a fascination it has never had since. But it is also clear that so far from the college as a whole having any responsibility for the disastrous course they engaged in, the vast majority of us opposed it — some of us, passionately — all the way along. We have seen that even the closest friends and associates of the appeasers did not agree with them. Brand, for example, who had largely helped in bringing Dawson back to *The Times*, constantly warned — and to no more effect than I, unimportant junior as I knew I was. Amery, we have seen, had a more consistently right attitude than anyone in politics, even than Churchill. Yet their attitude to him was a curious one; they regarded him as both a bit of a light-weight and also a bit heavy in the hand, something of a right-wing doctrinaire and curiously independent. A brave man, he had his own personal tragedy to live with all those years ; he never complained, he was a stoic and a most lovable man.

It was more remarkable that Lionel Curtis should never have been carried away by his friends', particularly Lothian's, crazy nonsense about Germany. It is odd that he should have had any defence-mechanism against it ; that he had was not only due to virtue. Lionel was a man of one idea, or rather of intense concentration on very few ideas, which he then regarded as more important than anything else in the world : he was their Prophet. But foreign affairs were not his concern, except for his sentimental friendship with Helmuth von Moltke. When the catastrophe of the fall of France came, and I really thought we were done for, Lionel said to me, 'All that is left is that we must go down fighting'. 'Speak for yourself,' I thought, and aloud — 'this is what your friends have brought us to.'

At the height of these events the celibate Salter chose to get married. At this, his college-servant, who had never been able to make much of him, expressed his opinion : 'Wonders'll never cease. First, the fall of France, and now — this!' Life in college in those days was not without its amusing aspects — after all this wise-acre's vote was as good as anybody else's, and he had done less damage to the country than some of the most eminent among the Fellows.

One profound reason both for the so-called National Government's electoral invincibility from 1931 onwards and for its lack of convictions was that by the ambivalence of its nature it was able to appeal to many Liberals as well as to the Conservatives who provided its majority. It was impossible ever to throw it out — only a national disaster could do that, as events proved.

One of the college Liberals who thus found his opportunity in 1931 was Donald Somervell. A personally charming man, who served throughout the first war, he was elected from Magdalen in 1912 and remained a Fellow most of his life. As a lawyer he did not have any responsibility for policy; but he was a consistent Chamberlainite all the way along, a smooth advocate — with no more knowledge of Europe and European history than the rest of them — of the absurd course they were on. I well remember how irritated he would be at any challenging of this course by a junior like me. But his complacency — he considered Munich 'a miracle of timing' — more than irritated me: I grew to dislike him for it. The graver the situation was, the airier he became — as another college lawyer, of greater ability and penetration, observed.

It is true that Somervell was not a political leader, but merely a Government lawyer. Elected as they all were of this vast, unprincipled majority in 1931, Somervell became a law-officer as Solicitor General in 1933 and there he remained all through everything till the end in 1945. Even then, even after the experience of serving in Churchill's heroic war-time government, his sentiments were by no means favourable to Churchill: not far beneath lay the animus of the true Chamberlainite. And underneath the polite surface of Conservatism, there is a good deal of that still. Such people will not relish being reminded of their responsibilities and fatuities by this book.

One of the college ecclesiastics, Bishop Headlam of Gloucester, was occasionally moved to emit pro-German sentiments in the papers — no doubt under the influence of his half-German nephew and niece. The latter, Agnes Headlam-Morley, subsequently promoted Professor of International Relations, was a constant protagonist of these views through thick and thin, whom nothing that the

Germans did would ever dissuade. This difference of opinion never affected my relations with Headlam, which were indeed those of mutual affection, especially later when we came to share rooms together.

On the other hand, I did not derive much amusement from the society of Hubert Henderson. Successor to D. H. MacGregor in the chair of economics, he was a recruit from outside and, an ex-Liberal, he was a natural and convinced Chamberlainite. I had displeasing arguments with him — all the more so in that he was an economist, and as a Labour candidate I was tied up to the nonsense of socialist economics I never believed in. Too much horse-sense: 'the nationalisation of the means of production, distribution and exchange', to be sure! Could one see those people running industry, or the banks, or the land, who couldn't even run a whelk-stall ? I remember Oman saying to me once that never in Parliament's history had there been so many members incapable of earning £600 a year any other way. This just reflection did not put me much in love with the intellectual standards of my party. And I may as well say that, with my belief in incentive, initiative, hard work, and with no illusions about people's average capacities, or the humbug of the welfare-state, I should have had no valid reason for not being a Conservative, if it had not been for the ruinous foreign policy they pursued in the 1930's. Churchillian Conservatism I could have found no valid reason for opposing; I agreed with both its terms : both its economics, by no means reactionary but not losing touch with the ground of common sense, or its foreign policy, rooted in the sense of the security of the country and of Europe. What kept me a

Labour man in all those years was simply the fatal course of Baldwin and Chamberlain's foreign policy. The Labour Party — for all the lunatic fringe it had to carry, of pacifists and illusionists — did stand for collective security ; and that to me — as it was to Churchill and others — was a concept of which the essence and the force was the Grand Alliance. This was the only thing that Hitler feared, the realisation of which would have put paid to his career. But it was the one course the National Government would not pursue ; they pursued the opposite, 'understanding' with Germany, until the end.

Henderson actually had the hardihood to defend the Chamberlainite course in argument : I can see him now, physically tying himself in knots, his right hand running through his hair. No doubt, to do him justice, my feeling was rather '*cet animal est très méchant, quand on l'attaque il se défend*'. All the same, he was the only man of them all I did not like, save for Zulueta. I suppose allowances should be made for this man who was *ur*-Basque on one side and Irish on the other. The be-all and end-all of his politics was just that Franco might win. A good classical scholar and learned in the civil law, he was one of the most obtuse men I have ever come across. He did confess to me one day that he simply could not understand the English, or their ways of mind (in that like Belloc) ; and I don't wonder.

An opposite number to him among his law-colleagues, opposite in every sense, was J. L. Brierly, Professor of International Law. A man of much sensitiveness and refinement, of a discriminating judgment, an international lawyer of distinction, he was a convinced supporter of collective security. He was, indeed, a Labour man. Too sensitive, and somewhat wanting in force, he had twice been the candidate of the younger generation for the wardenship ; after his second rebuff he did not feel the same about the college and rather withdrew from its life.

One who had been Simon's candidate for the wardenship after Anson died was Sir Charles Grant Robertson, who went on to something altogether more important and became a memorable Vice-Chancellor of Birmingham University. But he continued to play a full part in the life of the college to his last days, and no-one had a more staunch or consistent record against Chamberlainism. It was brave of him, considering his relation to the Chamberlains in Birmingham, and he risked his friendship with Neville by saying outright and in public what he thought of his appeasement policy. As the author of what is still the best biography of Bismarck, he knew what was what about the Germans. A celebrated lecturer in his day, whose conversation was interesting if insensitive, for he carried the lecturing habit into the common-room, he had a certain nobility of nature, and candour of spirit. He was not afraid to speak out : I not only agreed with him, but regarded him with respect and teasing affection.

It was Robertson who appointed another All Souls man, Keith Hancock, to the chair of modern history at Birmingham. A gifted historian, Hancock may be thought of along with Reggie Coupland, for the central field of his interest was in Empire and Commonwealth history and he wrote a masterly *Survey of Commonwealth Affairs*. An Australian Rhodes scholar, he was an obvious recruit to the Rhodes and

Round Table group. But as the appeasement policy of its leading members became more and more insupportable, he quietly resigned and withdrew.

Of other academic Fellows I could wish that E. L. Woodward [1] and G. N. Clark had spoken out : they both knew the truth about the Germans. Feiling did not : he was the only one among the historians who regularly defended the Chamberlainite course.

As for the younger generation then in college we were fiercely, desperately, against it. There were my particular and closest friends, Richard Pares and Geoffrey Hudson, A. H. M. Jones and A. H. Campbell, Ian Bowen, Isaiah Berlin and Douglas Jay. We all loathed and detested it, and saw perfectly well where it was all leading. Even Quintin Hogg (now Lord Hailsham), who was elected member for Oxford City in the year of Munich, was not really a Chamberlainite ; he was naturally a Churchillian. As for the youngest of the Fellows, Dick Latham and Harry Davies— the former an Australian who would have made a name if he had lived — both, alas, were lost at sea : Latham in the R.A.F., Davies in the Royal Navy.

How to account for this prolonged aberration of the most eminent ?

It is indeed a strange case, and takes some explaining : yet it has its historical significance, and was something of a symptom, a pointer to the future too. These men came at the end of an age ; they were late Victorians by birth

[1] Especially, perhaps, Woodward, whose *Great Britain and the German Navy* reveals irrefutably the responsibility of the Germans for the naval challenge to Britain's very existence that led to the war of 1914–18.

and upbringing, sharing to the full the standards of that era, with all their limitations, public-spirited and respectable, conventional and unimaginative. Indeed, they distrusted imagination and intellectualism ; it was not good form to hammer things out in discussion, perhaps even to think things out. The contrast here with Churchill is very marked. *The Times History* bears this out in Dawson, the most powerful man of them all. 'His remarkable capacity to decide quickly the innumerable questions that present themselves every day was accompanied by a strong reluctance to discuss in detail the serious questions of the time. In conversation it was imperative that such questions be handled lightly. If anyone attempted to entrap him in discussion, or hold forth to him, he was swift in closing the interview. Those in professional contact with him were soon made conscious of particular forms of Dawsonian disapproval. Those lacking a hereditary sense of social tact were briefly dealt with. It was a serious obstacle to a man's progress in the office if he were so unfortunate as to qualify for the description of "Bore".' [1]

That is completely accurate. As I observed Dawson, I regarded him as an empiricist, with no principles, properly speaking, to guide him in a world profoundly changing, where the Victorian landmarks were toppling over, their values inapplicable. What was the point of attaching so much importance to social convention ? (He used to observe of one Cabinet, half-humorously, that it had all too few Etonians, and not one 'wet-bob' among them — but it was only *half*-humorously.)

[1] *History*, 799.

G. M. Trevelyan has several times suggested one line of explanation for them — there is no excuse — and that perhaps the fairest and best. These decent good men did not know what kind of men they were dealing with in Hitler and his kind. I dare say that is true. But they were told often enough : why would they not take telling ?

This leads us nearer the heart of the problem.

As I have said, they were ignorant of Europe and European history ; they had read Greats at Oxford, then Dawson went to South Africa and Simon to the Bar. All this group knew more about the Empire than they did about Europe, or the world. In addition, some of them were much influenced by Cecil Rhodes's insistent (and ignorant) pro-Germanism.

There is a further consideration of some interest for political thought — or for those who are interested in English processes of political thought. In this story we see the decadence of British empiricism, empiricism carried beyond all rhyme or reason. In general I am in sympathy with empiricism in politics ; I much prefer it to doctrinairism. The practical way of looking at things, not looking too far in advance (*pace* Amery), not rocking the boat, and other clichés that do duty for thinking ahead, may serve well enough in ordinary, normal times. But our times are not 'normal' in the good old Victorian sense, and never will be again. And this habit of mind in politics will certainly not serve in times of revolution, perpetual stress and conflict, war, the reshaping of the world. This conventional British way of looking at things was simply not equal to the times, and it caught these men out badly.

Even so, the empirical habit of mind, that considered itself so much more practical — E. H. Carr in his writings at the time thought these people more 'realist' in their estimate of Hitler! — need not have equated itself with ignorance. Not one of these men in high place in those years ever so much as read *Mein Kampf*, or would listen to anybody who had. They really did not know what they were dealing with, or the nature and degree of the evil thing they were up against. To be so uninstructed — a condition that arose in part from a certain superciliousness, a lofty smugness, as well as superficiality of mind — was in itself a kind of dereliction of duty.

They would not listen to warnings, because they did not wish to hear. And they did not think things out, because there was a fatal confusion in their minds between the interests of their social order and the interests of their country. They did not say much about it, since that would have given the game away, and anyway it was a thought they did not wish to be too explicit about even to themselves, but they were anti-Red and that hamstrung them in dealing with the greater immediate danger to their country, Hitler's Germany.

There is a rider to add to this point about class. These men, even Halifax, were essentially middle-class, not aristocrats. They did not have the hereditary sense of the security of the state, unlike Churchill, Eden, the Cecils. Nor did they have the toughness of the 18th-century aristocracy. They came at the end of the ascendancy of the Victorian middle-class, deeply affected as that was by high-mindedness and humbug. They all talked, in one form or another, the language of disingenuousness and cant : it was second nature to them — so different from Churchill. This, and the essential pettiness of the National Government, all flocking together to keep Labour out, was deeply corrupting, both to them and the nation. It meant that they failed to see what was true, until too late, when it was simply a question of survival.

What I had under observation, then, in all those years was a class in decadence. These eminent specimens of it, be-ribboned and be-coroneted — all except Dawson, who, as editor of *The Times*, was above such things — with the best will in the world well-nigh ruined their country and reduced it to a second-rate place in the world.

The total upshot of their efforts was to aid Nazi-Germany to achieve a position of brutal ascendancy, a threat to everybody else's security or even existence, which only a war could end. This had the very result of letting the Russians into the centre of Europe which the appeasers — so far as they had any clear idea of policy — wished to prevent. Of course their responsibility was a secondary one. The primary responsibility was all along that of the Germans : the people in the strongest strategic position in Europe, the keystone of the whole European system, but who never knew how to behave, whether up or down, in the ascendant arrogant and brutal, in defeat base and grovelling.

These men had no real conception of Germany's character or malign record in modern history. Quite simply, we owe the wreck of Europe's position in the world to Germany's total inability to play her proper rôle in it.

That was no reason why these Englishmen should —

largely out of ignorance and confusion of mind — have done everything to aid the process ; in the event bringing down the British Empire with it too, for which they cared infinitely more than ever they did for Europe or Europe's place in the world.

SOME CHARACTERS

AMERY, LEOPOLD S., 1873–1955. Educated : Harrow, Balliol. Elected Fellow of All Souls, 1897. On the staff of *The Times*, 1899–1909 ; *Times* war correspondent in South Africa, 1899–1900. M.P., 1911–45. Served in Flanders and the Near East, 1914–16. Assistant Secretary to the War Cabinet, 1917. Under-Secretary of State for the Colonies, 1919–21 ; Secretary of State for the Colonies, 1924–9, and for Dominion Affairs, 1925–9. First Lord of the Admiralty, 1922–4. Secretary of State for India, 1940–45.

  Among his books, *The Times History of the South African War*, 7 vols. ; *The Empire in the New Era*, 1928 ; *My Political Life*, 3 vols., 1953 and later.

BARRINGTON-WARD, ROBERT M., 1891–1948. Educated : Westminster, Balliol. Editorial Secretary to *The Times*, 1913. Served throughout the war in France and Belgium, 1914–19. Assistant Editor of *The Observer*, 1919–27 ; Assistant Editor of *The Times*, 1927–41 ; Editor of *The Times*, 1941–8.

BALDWIN, STANLEY, 1ST EARL, 1867–1947. Educated : Harrow, Trinity College, Cambridge. M.P., 1908–37. Financial Secretary to the Treasury, 1917–21. President of the Board of Trade, 1922. Chancellor of the Exchequer, 1922–3. Prime Minister, 1923–4, 1924–9, 1935–7. Lord President of the Council, 1931–5. Chancellor of Cambridge University from 1930.

  Among his publications, *Peace and Goodwill in Industry*,

1925 ; *On England and other Addresses*, 1926 ; *Our Inheritance* (Speeches), 1928 ; *This Torch of Freedom* (more Speeches), 1935 ; *Service of Our Lives*, 1937 ; *An Interpreter of England*, 1939.

BRAND, ROBERT H., 1ST BARON, 1878–   . Educated : Marlborough, New College. Elected Fellow of All Souls, 1902. Served in South Africa under Lord Milner, Lord Selborne and General Botha, 1902–9. Secretary to the Transvaal delegation at the South African National Convention, 1908–9. Member of the Imperial Munitions Board, Canada, 1915–18. Financial representative of South Africa, Genoa Conference, 1922 ; member of Expert Committee advising the German government on stabilisation of the mark, 1922. Member of the Macmillan Committee on Finance and Industry, 1931. Head of the British Food Mission, Washington, 1941–4. Representative of the Treasury in Washington, 1944–6. Director of Lazard Brothers, of The Times Publishing Co., and of Lloyds Bank.

Among his books, *The Union of South Africa*, 1909.

CHAMBERLAIN, NEVILLE, 1869–1940. Educated : Rugby, Birmingham. Growing sisal in the Bahamas, 1890–7. Entered Birmingham City Council, 1911 ; Lord Mayor, 1915–16. Director-General of National Service, 1916–17. Postmaster General, 1922–23 ; Paymaster-General, 1923. Minister of Health, 1923, 1924–9, 1931. Chancellor of the Exchequer, 1923–4, 1931–7. Prime Minister, 1937–40. Lord President of the Council, 1940.

COUPLAND, SIR REGINALD, 1884–1952. Educated : Winchester, New College. Fellow of Trinity, 1907–14 ; Beit Lecturer in Colonial History, 1913–18 ; Beit Professor of the History of the British Empire at Oxford, 1920–48 ; Fellow of All Souls, 1920–48, 1952. Editor of *The Round Table*, 1917–19, 1939–41. Member of the Royal Commission on the Indian Civil Service, 1923. Adviser to the Burma Round Table Conference, 1931. Member of the Palestine Royal

Commission, 1936–7. Member of Sir Stafford Cripps's Mission to India, 1942.

Among his many admirable books, *The American Revolution and the British Empire*, 1930 ; *The British Anti-Slavery Movement*, 1933 ; *The British Empire in These Days*, 1935 ; *Kirk on the Zambesi*, 1928 ; *East Africa and its Invaders*, 1938 ; *The Exploitation of East Africa*, 1939 ; *The Cripps Mission*, 1942 ; *The Indian Problem*, 1942 ; *Indian Politics*, 1943 ; *India: A Re-Statement*, 1945 ; *Livingstone's Last Journey*, 1945.

CURTIS, LIONEL, 1872–1955. Educated : Haileybury, New College. Served in the South African War, 1899–1900 ; acting Town Clerk of Johannesburg, from 1901. Assistant Colonial Secretary to the Transvaal, 1907. Founded *The Round Table*. Adviser on Irish Affairs to the Colonial Office, 1921–4. Elected Fellow of All Souls, 1921. Founded the Royal Institute of International Affairs.

Among his books, *The Problem of the Commonwealth*, 1916 ; *Dyarchy* (India), 1920 ; *The Capital Question of China*, 1932 ; *Civitas Dei*, 3 vols., 1934–7 ; *With Milner in South Africa*, 1951.

DAWSON, GEOFFREY, 1874–1944. Assumed name of Dawson by Royal Licence instead of Robinson, on inheriting a Yorkshire estate. Educated : Eton, Magdalen. Elected Fellow of All Souls, 1899. In the Colonial Office, 1898–1901. Private Secretary to Lord Milner in South Africa, 1901–5. Editor of the *Johannesburg Star*, 1905–10. Editor of *The Times*, 1912–19, and 1923–41. In the interval, Estates Bursar of All Souls, 1919–23. Secretary to the Rhodes Trust, 1921–22 ; Rhodes Trustee from 1925.

HALIFAX, 1ST EARL OF, EDWARD, 1881–1959. Educated : Eton, Christ Church. Elected Fellow of All Souls, 1904. M.P., 1910–25. Under-Secretary of State for the Colonies, 1921–1922. President of the Board of Education, 1922–4. Minister of Agriculture, 1924–5. Viceroy of India, 1926–31. President of the Board of Education, 1932–5. Secretary of

State for War, 1935. Lord Privy Seal, 1935-7. Leader of the House of Lords, 1935-8, 1940. Lord President of the Council, 1937-8. Secretary of State for Foreign Affairs, 1938-40. British Ambassador in Washington, 1941-6. Chancellor of Oxford University, 1933-59.

His *Speeches* were edited by his colleague in the election of 1904 at All Souls, Sir Edmund Craster.

HOARE, SAMUEL, 1ST VISCOUNT TEMPLEWOOD, 1880-1959. Educated : Harrow, New College. Assistant Secretary to the Colonial Secretary, 1905. M.P., 1910-44. Secretary of State for Air, 1922-4, 1924-9, 1940. Secretary of State for India, 1931-5. Secretary of State for Foreign Affairs, 1935. First Lord of the Admiralty, 1936-7. Secretary of State for Home Affairs, 1937-9. Lord Privy Seal, 1939-40. Ambassador to Spain, 1940-44.

JONES, THOMAS, 1870-1955. Educated : Pengam County School; University College, Aberystwyth ; Glasgow University ; London School of Economics. Secretary to the National Health Insurance Commissioners (Wales), 1912-16. Deputy Secretary to the Cabinet, 1916-30. Secretary to the Economic Advisory Council. Secretary to the Pilgrim Trust, 1930-45 ; Trustee, 1945 ; Chairman, 1952-4.

LOTHIAN, 11TH MARQUIS OF, PHILIP KERR, 1882-1940. Educated: The Oratory School, Birmingham, New College. Assistant Secretary to the Intercolonial Council in the Transvaal, 1905-8. Editor of *The Round Table*, 1910-16. Secretary to the Prime Minister, 1916-21. Secretary to the Rhodes Trust, 1925-39. Chancellor of the Duchy of Lancaster, 1931. Under-Secretary of State for India, 1931-2. British Ambassador to Washington, 1939-40.

Owned about 28,000 acres ; frequent contributor to *The Times* and the *Observer*.

ROBERTSON, SIR CHARLES GRANT, 1869-1948. Educated : Highgate School, Hertford College. Elected Fellow of All Souls, 1893 ; Domestic Bursar, 1897-1920, 1940-4. Principal,

1920–38, and Vice-Chancellor, 1927–38, of Birmingham University.

Wrote, among other books, the best English biography of Bismarck.

SALTER, ARTHUR, 1ST BARON, 1881– . Educated : Oxford High School, Brasenose College. Entered Admiralty, 1904. Assistant Secretary to the National Health Insurance Commission, 1913. Director of Ship Requisitioning, 1917. Secretary to Allied Maritime Transport Council, 1918. General Secretary to the Reparations Commission, 1920–2. Director, Economic Section of the League of Nations, 1919–1920, 1922–31. Missions to India, 1930, China, 1931, 1933. Professor of Political Theory and Institutions, Oxford, 1934–1944. Elected Fellow of All Souls, 1934. Parliamentary Secretary to the Ministry of Shipping, 1939–41. Head of British Merchant Shipping Mission to Washington, 1941–3. Chancellor of the Duchy of Lancaster, 1945. M.P. for Oxford University, 1937–50 ; for Ormskirk, 1951–3. Minister for Economic Affairs, 1951–2. Minister of Materials, 1952–3.

Among his books, *Allied Shipping Control*, 1921 ; *Recovery*, 1932 ; *Security*, 1939.

SIMON, JOHN, 1ST VISCOUNT, 1873–1954. Educated : Fettes, Wadham College. Elected Fellow of All Souls, 1897. M.P., 1906–18, 1922–40. Solicitor-General, 1910–13. Attorney-General, 1913–15. Secretary of State for Home Affairs, 1915–16, 1935–7. Secretary of State for Foreign Affairs, 1931–5. Chancellor of the Exchequer, 1937–40. Lord Chancellor, 1940–5. High Steward of Oxford University.

SOMERVELL, DONALD, 1ST BARON, 1889–1960. Educated: Harrow, Magdalen College. Elected Fellow of All Souls, 1912. Served throughout the war, 1914–19. M.P. 1931–45. Solicitor-General, 1933–36. Attorney-General, 1936–45. Home Secretary, 1945. Lord Justice of Appeal, 1946–54.